To Steve Meredith,
Best wishes and good luck

Dave Hill

TEED OFF

TEED OFF

by Dave Hill
and Nick Seitz

PRENTICE-HALL, INC., Englewood Cliffs, N.J.

TEED OFF by Dave Hill and Nick Seitz

Copyright © 1977 by Dave Hill and Nick Seitz

Printed in the United States of America

Prentice-Hall International, Inc., London
Prentice-Hall of Australia, Pty. Ltd., Sydney
Prentice-Hall of Canada, Ltd., Toronto
Prentice-Hall of India Private Ltd., New Delhi
Prentice-Hall of Japan, Inc., Tokyo
Prentice-Hall of Southeast Asia Pte. Ltd., Singapore
Whitehall Books Limited, Wellington, New Zealand

10 9 8 7 6 5

Library of Congress Cataloging in Publication Data

Hill, Dave
   Teed off.

   1. Hill, Dave,   2. Golf—United States.
3. Golfers—United States—Biography.   I. Seitz,
Nick,   joint author. II. Title.
GV964.H46A37   796.352'092'4 [B]   76–30769
ISBN 0–13–902247–3

CONTENTS

INTRODUCTION

As a golf writer and editor I've always been partial to Dave Hill for a selfish reason—he's great copy. He's opinionated, fearless, and funny, if not necessarily in that order.

A paint company conducted a poll a few years ago to determine the most colorful player on the tour (ouch) and Hill won. I voted for him and explained, "He keeps me awake."

The most controversial player in a game that attracts strong personalities, he attributes his image largely to the press, claiming that most of his incendiary remarks have come in reply to reporters' questions. Dave Hill has never been one to dodge a provocative question. If they don't want a forthright answer, he says, they shouldn't ask him. If he is fined for his forthrightness, well, it's only money.

In putting together this book over the past three years, I must have asked Dave five thousand questions, about everything from the superstars, to course design, to sex, and he invariably was ready with quick but reasoned responses. I think the result is the most candid, probing book about the tour we have seen. Frank Beard wrote a lively diary of a year on tour and submitted it for review to Joe Dey, commissioner at that time. Dey deleted a number of outspoken passages. Dave's book has gone only to lawyers, who checked it for libel. (His own brother is a lawyer but declined to get involved.)

I think several aspects of Dave's attitude have been over-looked and should be pointed up at the outset. One is his sense of humor. Much of what he says, while on his verbal target, is said with tongue in cheek. Sometimes it's protruding visibly. But that humor gets lost when a headline writer a thousand miles away pulls a spicy quote out of context and overplays it. It doesn't bother Dave. It does, I learned, bother his mother, a sprightly, white-haired woman with a fine sense of the ridiculous herself. Both of them enjoy kidding people who take themselves too seriously. The golf tour is crowded with such people. Hill hasn't forgotten that golf is just a game, not a world war.

Also ignored is the fact that Hill often says what the greats of the game are thinking—but are afraid to express. After Hill sounded off about Hazeltine, a poor U.S. Open course, Arnold Palmer told him, "You stole my lines." Hill says he wishes Palmer had spoken out because the criticism would have meant more coming from Palmer.

And his outspokenness has all but obscured Hill's perfectionist approach to golf. Knowing both of them reasonably well, I would suggest that Hill's dedication to understanding golf technique and equipment comes closer than any contemporary player to that of the immortal Ben Hogan. I have seen Hill take a 7-iron to dinner in a posh restaurant trying to work out the pressure points of his grip.

He may well be the best shotmaker on the tour today, a testimony to the hundreds of thousands of practice balls he has hit since he was a youngster. I know of no shot he has not mastered or could not improvise if necessary. He has per-

viii

fected delicate little specialty shots—like blading the ball in the belly with a sand wedge when it's up against the collar of a green—that soon were adopted by other top pros.

Frank Thomas, the resident technical expert of the United States Golf Association, says Hill hits more shots on the sweet spot of the clubface than anybody else in the game. To Hill the Vardon Trophy for the low stroke average is the most telling award in golf, because it rewards shotmaking consistency. He was saying so before he won it in 1969.

Hill has driven himself and cultivated a power game to go with his control, although he weighs only slightly more than his golf umbrella. With his temperament, he says, if he were any bigger he'd be in jail or dead. He adds that he has had 400 fistfights, has won none of them, and, should he ever find the man he can whip, he would sign him up and take him around the country with him. "I'm crazy," Hill concludes, "but I have an advantage over most people. I know it."

George Low, a shrewd enough judge of people to be able to travel the tour in high style without working for a living, gives a more serious assessment. "I'll take Hill over any of 'em for a stand-up guy," he says. So will I.

Nick Seitz

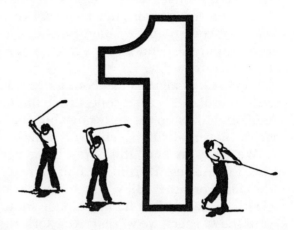

INGRATES

The average touring pro today is living off the fat of the land and thinks the world owes him $200,000 a year. Most golf pros couldn't do anything else for a living, but they always have their hands out looking for a freebie. Instead of saying "Thank you" they want to know what time the next plane is leaving.

They forget that we're playing a game. All of us could drop dead tomorrow and the world wouldn't be any worse off. Our relative importance is pretty insignificant. It's too bad the Kennedy brothers and Martin Luther King were killed, because they were contributing to society. The golf pro doesn't contribute much.

Golf has become too big a business. There's too much money. The players are businessmen instead of athletes, and the enjoyment is going out of the tour, for us and for the fans.

Frank Beard is always saying he doesn't get any fun out of the game because it's a job and he's playing for a lot of money.

1

The course is his office and he can't be disturbed. If Beard doesn't enjoy the game, he ought to go work for a living for the first time in his life and see how he likes that! Let him carry mail for a year or work in a factory. I've done those things. It can give you an appreciation for the soft life. These touring pros ought to spend a year working in a pro shop at a club, twelve hours a day.

I get sick of all the talk about money. I'd like to start every season broke. Then I'd concentrate on the game. I've made a million dollars on the tour now, but that doesn't make me a great player—I still haven't won a major championship.

We are lucky enough to draw big galleries, but the players shut themselves off from the fans. The players get all upset if the fans breathe. Billy Casper is always hearing camera clicks—usually when he hits a poor shot. The week after he won the Masters, we were in New Orleans and a cameraman was shooting Billy and our group. Billy climbed all over him. Billy had just won what I consider the most important tournament in golf. I told him if I ever win the Masters, you could drive over me with a steamroller the next week.

Bruce Crampton is always glaring and snapping at fans because they aren't doing perfect imitations of the Statue of Liberty while he's preparing to make a deathless shot. He has a running war with photographers; they aren't supposed to be seen, let alone heard. My attitude is that if you have that much trouble concentrating, maybe you're playing the wrong game.

Golf pros have been spoiled with silence over the years, but those days are disappearing. We're getting more bleacher fans like the team sports. Instead of confiscating their banners and buttons, we should be welcoming their interest. (You never saw signs banned from the course until the ones that said "Hill's Angels," as I recall.)

Most fans are generous with their applause. I love them for their enthusiasm. It pumps me up and I play better. I don't draw big galleries—a few years ago you could get all my followers on the back of a motorcycle—but crowds are so big at many tournaments that they're packed around every tee and green.

I often wonder why the fans put up with all the abuse to watch us. You walk a mile from your car to the course and you walk around the course following the action. At most tournaments there are no grandstands. You have to stand in a long line to get a hot dog which probably costs a buck. For all this you pay $5 to $10. And then some smart-assed golf pro snaps at you because you rattled some change in your pocket.

It would be nice for us if there were no distractions, but with several hundred people crowded around a green, somebody is going to shake the ice in his drink cup and make a little noise. We might just as well get used to it if we want to play for more money. If we expect distractions, they don't bother us as much. It's the cough that breaks a complete silence that unnerves a player when he's drawing back the putter. If everybody were coughing we'd get used to it.

Greensboro has the noisiest galleries on the tour, and some players refuse to play there. I usually enjoy Greensboro because the fans are having so much fun. They can be nasty. Charlie Sifford has had some bad experiences with people piling beer cans on top of his ball and calling him a no-good nigger. But that's rare. Out of 45,000 people, most of them are just down-to-earth, ordinary workers out for a good time. They bring their buckets of beer and laugh and giggle and bet on everything that comes off the clubface. They'll congregate around a par-3 hole like the sixteenth, which is too long for the size of the green and sometimes calls for a driver, and they'll bet on "greenies"—that is, on who can hit the green. When you get on the green, they'll bet on the putts. You're liable to miss a six-footer and hear some guy who works in a furniture factory holler, "You dumb SOB, you just cost me a quarter."

If you can share the mood with them, it's very funny. You

3

aren't going to change them, so you might just as well join in. I yell back at them and ask them for a beer. It's like being at the circus. They eat and drink and have a big time and forget their troubles. They definitely do not come to the tournament to be chewed out by the entertainers.

One thing we could do is answer fans' questions during a round, within reason. Most of these people play golf and they are curious about what kind of shot I am playing and what club I am using. They're comparing their games with mine. I don't think it hurts a player to turn around and give a short answer to a question about his shot, even if he didn't hit it super. Then the fan won't go home and tell everybody in his neighborhood what a bunch of temperamental types the golf pros are.

Sure, a lot of fans are stupid. They just follow Jack Nicklaus or whoever is hot. They judge only the results, not the type of shot played. They applaud bad shots and don't applaud good ones because they don't know the difference.

You know, if I put it in the trees and the ball's sitting up and I have a six-foot opening, I have a dead easy shot. And yet, to people standing around watching, it's a very difficult shot. I might have to cut or draw the shot a little, but that's nothing to a pro. Some pros bleed that sort of situation for all the drama it's worth, but there's no problem there.

On the other hand, a tough shot would be when the ball is in long grass, a poor lie, and you have to hit it under a tree limb and then clear a bunker and stop the ball quickly on the green. You can't stop the ball hitting it low out of long grass. I'd prefer to be playing that shot off bare ground.

But fans are getting smarter about the game all the time. They read about it and watch it on television. Golf is the only game where the fans can be standing right next to their favorite players in the middle of the action. I don't think we have to give golf lessons, but we could explain before we hit a shot what we're going to try to do with it and why, and what

4

club we're going to use. The player could explain that he is going to try to keep the ball to the right of the flag with a fade because the wind is blowing from right to left and the trouble is on the left. That doesn't take much time and energy. One of the television networks has been experimenting with announcers on the fairways. It's a great idea, but the golfers aren't talking to the announcers enough—and television directly supplies over a third of our purse money. We players forget we are entertainers. To us, golf is a business, but to the other 99.9 percent of the population that plays golf it's a game. I don't believe in entertaining the fans with a hot-dog vaudeville routine, but I think we can entertain them by telling them what we're trying to do on the course. We can entertain them by giving autographs on the course when it doesn't interrupt play. We don't have anything better to do between shots. It takes five seconds to sign an autograph.

We can also entertain the fans by staging clinics after play is over. The players could take turns participating. If I'm good with a pitching wedge, I could give the pitching wedge part. At the end we could have questions from the audience. The players used to do more of this sort of thing in the old days. They promoted the tour then and built it so that we can get rich today, but we don't ever give them credit for it. The old long driving contests were good entertainment, but now we don't want to bother.

In the old days the fans were free to roam around the course. They weren't restrained by ropes everywhere they turned. Jimmy Demaret tells me we ought to burn all the ropes. I don't think that's practical with the bigger galleries today, but his point about making the fans feel more appreciated is sound.

The fans who really hold the tour together are the volunteer workers at each tournament. Literally hundreds of them drive the courtesy cars, keep score, marshal. And how do the big-shot players treat them? Frequently without even a "thank

5

you." A player like Bruce Crampton always seems to be bawling out a marshal for some terrible offense such as scratching his nose at the wrong time. The marshal is probably the president of a local bank, who's on vacation and who's bought a $500 sponsorship to help his home town tournament. Next year he's liable to save himself the misery.

Most players treat pro-am day, which raises a lot of money for the tournament, with all the affection they give pneumonia. They mope around the course barely talking to their amateur partners, who have paid maybe $1,500 for the privilege of being snubbed. It's a big thrill for the amateurs to be playing with the pros. They love to get a golf tip from a pro. They'll talk about it at work for months and be the envy of their weekend foursomes.

The pro-am can be a pain in the butt, especially if you get a very serious team of amateurs who are determined to win and who forget to have fun. I look on the pro-am as a necessary evil that has some advantages. The profits are going to the purse and to charity. It gives me a chance to check my yardages before the tournament. I can meet influential people who might be able to help my career off the course. And it gives me a chance to walk around in the sun and play golf with some nice folks, which would be my first choice for something to do anyway.

Mainly the pro-am is helping the sponsor, who is usually in a financial bind. The poor sponsor has been struggling for months to raise money and we players don't have to do anything until Wednesday of tournament week! It costs just twice the purse total to put on a tour event today. Some of the players seem to think the sponsor is putting up all that money so he personally can watch them perform. Well, if all he wants to do is watch a golf pro, he can pick the best player in the world, pay him $15,000 and have him all to himself for a day.

We don't have that many good sponsors and we'd better be thinking of ways to help them. Two or three of us could go into a city a couple of months ahead of time to promote a tournament. We could play an exhibition and appear at a cocktail party and dinner. We could take turns and pay our own expenses. That would show the sponsor we have his interest in mind. We wouldn't just be coming to town for one week and running off with the money.

If we put our minds to it there are a lot of little things we could do. We all get three dozen new balls every week. After a tournament they're still like new. We could clean them up, autograph them, and throw them into a big box for the sponsor to sell. He'd certainly get a dollar a ball.

The biggest thing the players can do for a sponsor, of course, is play in his tournament. Too many of us avoid too many tournaments. Jack Nicklaus is the best player we have, and I wish he would play in more tournaments that need someone like him.

Jack is not an ungenerous man. One year he gave his first prize from his Kings Island Tournament to charity. But it's much easier for a multimillionaire to give his money than his time. Toward the end of the year most of his earnings probably go to the government in taxes anyway.

Jack always has avoided tournaments like Philadelphia, Sutton, Hartford, Milwaukee, Pensacola, Phoenix, and Tucson. He likes courses that suit his game and these don't. He can afford to be choosy. But is that in the best interest of golf? How would you like to be a sponsor scratching together $200,000 for a tournament every year and have to go without the great Jack Nicklaus time after time? I'll wager that Jack wasn't pleased when several players skipped his new Memorial Tournament last year. I was one of them. I didn't think a new tournament deserved prime Memorial Day weekend dates. We have loyal old sponsors who would have loved that slot, but Deane Beman, the commissioner, gave it to his old pal Jack.

Every player should play in every tournament at least once

every three years. He can rotate the ones he doesn't like. But he owes that much to the sponsors. I try to play in every tournament at least once each three years. I don't always do it, though. I'm like the big names—I prefer to play where I have fun and play well. I've never done any good in Dallas or Fort Worth. The girl-watching in Fort Worth is always better than my golf; it's the greatest show on tour.

In thirteen years at Dallas I doubt I've made over a thousand dollars. You feel you should play there because it's Byron Nelson's tournament. Byron is one of the old greats who built the tour in the days when the players had to push themselves off on radio stations and Lions Club lunches to sell tickets. We owe him something.

I think Gary Player and the other foreign players should have to play more than the prescribed 15 tournaments a year to keep their tour cards. I think they should have to play 25. Everybody realizes that Gary has a family in South Africa and likes to spend time at home, but he still has an obligation to the American tour. The whole tour, not just a small part of it. Gary comes to the United States only when he feels he is playing good golf. He plays the minimum number of tournaments, fills his sack, and goes back to South Africa. He prepares himself for several weeks and is at an advantage in the big championships. America is where he has made his money and reputation, and it's where his big endorsements are.

I'd like to see a little more gratitude from the foreign players. We've had foreign players come over here and knock everything in sight—Peter Thomson was the worst. He couldn't take our hamburger stands. What I don't understand is this: If they don't like it here, why don't they just stay home where it's so much better? The sponsors here deserve more support from foreign players, especially the ones who've gotten rich off of them. The sponsors deserve more support from all of us, myself included.

TOUR STRUCTURE

Even though Commissioner Deane Beman has designated a certain number of tournaments we must play, I would rather see a different plan to guarantee top players to all the sponsors on a rotating basis, and I think I know how it can be done. I have a feeling you could deliver the big-name players consistently if you guaranteed them money against their winnings. That's a far-out idea for golf but it's common in other businesses. That's the kind of deal I made to do this book: I got an advance against sales royalties.

Let's say you're a tournament sponsor. I want to be able to come to you and guarantee you 20 of the top 25 money winners every year. I want to give you their names well ahead of your tournament so you can use them to promote your ticket sales. The way it is now, except for the few "designated" tournaments, a sponsor might not know two weeks before his tournament starts whether he's going to have a Jack Nicklaus or a Jerry Pate. It would be like the New York Mets coming to town and nobody knowing if Tom Seaver will make the trip.

We go to Jack Nicklaus and say: "Jack, we have averaged

your tour income for the past five years and it comes to $185,000 a year. We are going to guarantee you $185,000 against your winnings next season. This gives us the right to assign you to play in ten tournaments. We'll give you plenty of notice so you can fit in all your side deals. Sign here."

Would the young players resent the guaranteed incomes going to Nicklaus and Player and a few others? A few probably would, but most of them ought to be smart enough to realize that the stars make it possible for them to make a good living. Without the top players there wouldn't be much of a tour.

The young players can see that a sponsor who loses money for two or three years is liable to toss in the towel. This business of hooking a high-powered commercial sponsor for a year and then losing him—Dow Jones was an example—isn't stable enough. A commercial sponsor can decide to shift his promotion money from golf to billboards. Some of the commercial sponsors are solid. But the civic sponsors are the staples and you have to take care of them. We've lost good tournaments in Portland and Seattle and we almost lost the Texas Open, which has been good to us in San Antonio for twenty years. You need a good balance between the commercial and the civic.

I've been laughed at for proposing a sliding purse scale that would depend on the caliber of the field, but that would be another way of looking out for our sponsors. A sponsor shouldn't have to offer $200,000 and wind up with a $75,000 field. He should know well in advance what players will be in his tournament, and if the field doesn't measure up he ought to be able to adjust his purse accordingly. It wouldn't be hard to work out a scale. A sponsor damn sure shouldn't have to put up a whopping purse if he gets only four of the top twenty money winners, should he? Right now we have the world by the tail, but it might not always be like this. If the economy nosedives, so will the golf tour.

10

I wouldn't be against appearance money for the top stars if the sponsor wants to give it. In the old days the stars got appearance money, sometimes above the table, sometimes under it. The sponsor should have the freedom to pay whomever he wants.

If a player is good for the gate, I say he deserves special considerations. Let the sponsor at least pick up his expenses for the week. It's done all the time by foreign tournaments. When I go to play in a foreign tournament I get a guarantee. Otherwise I wouldn't go.

I would guess that Nicklaus is worth 15,000 people to a typical tournament. Multiply that by, say, $7 a head and you have a sizable hunk of income for the sponsor.

A lot of people would like to cut the tour from forty-plus down to twenty or thirty events. Instead of trying to end the tour by Labor Day, we ought to be thinking about filling up the open dates in the fall with tournaments, to give the younger players a chance. Smaller tournaments if necessary, but tournaments. You develop your talent of the future by giving the young pros of today experience. I don't care how good a kid was as an amateur or how many hours he spends on the practice tee, he still isn't a golf pro until he's out here getting experience under pressure. We have over 300 guys trying to make a living at the tour and about 85 percent of them don't make their expenses every year. It costs at least $25,000 to travel the tour and that isn't living too royally. You might have a sponsor to pick up the tab but you still have to get competition.

We need a satellite tournament every week for the players who don't qualify for the regular field. I think we should subsidize these tournaments. In baseball the major leagues help underwrite the minor leagues. It should be the same in golf.

You could qualify 44 people out of this week's satellite

tournament for next week's big tournament. The other 100 in the big tournament would come from the money list. Those who aren't in the big tournament fall back into the satellite. Then you eliminate this awful Monday qualifying.

The way it is now, if a young guy misses qualifying on Monday he doesn't really get to compete again until the next Monday. He tries so damn hard to get into a tournament he can't play at all. Then if he does get in, he worries about making the cut so he won't have to qualify again the next week. It's tough.

I'm not saying we owe a living to every kid who can hit it 250 yards. About a hundred guys on tour have no business out here. I'd give them two years to make the top 100 and then say adios. But when we have a qualifying tournament to get on the tour and we give the top finishers cards that entitle them to play out here, we owe them the chance to play and develop their skills. Plenty of guys who are making big money today wouldn't have lasted on the tour if they'd had to buck all this Monday qualifying and competition when they first came out. It took a guy like Dale Douglass about six years on the tour to become a pro golfer and then he won tournaments. Today he'd be sent packing.

I don't think Deane Beman is too concerned about the young players. I think he's more concerned with building our television ratings. Maybe he figures that these independent mini-tours that have been springing up like mushrooms in the last few years can fill the gap for the young players. I'm dubious. Too many of the mini-tours have been started by fly-by-night guys you'd never buy a used car from.

Beman's grand scheme, which he thought up with Joe Dey, who had the job before him and chose him to be his successor, was to have a dozen or fifteen "designated tournaments" each year in which all the leading players would have to play. The players who did best overall in the designated events would qualify for a big championship at the end of the season, around Labor Day. It looks like the expanded World Series of Golf will become the big year-end finale.

Nicklaus and Palmer and Player grumbled about having to play in even three tournaments the first year. I don't think Beman will ever get his total of twelve or fifteen designateds. The stars won't swallow that much direction—unless you guarantee them money against their winnings.

The Tournament Players Championship is advertised as the fifth major championship. Right now it isn't, because it takes time to build a major championship. The press will make or break the tournament. The press has made the Masters a major title in a short time. If the TPC gets the backing of the press and if the permanent site at Jacksonville proves out, it could become a major event—in ten years or so.

Beman says the TPC isn't meant to rival the PGA Championship, but I have to wonder. The PGA has always been known as the pros' own championship—and now the TPC is trying to sell that line. The Tournament Players Division is still part of the main PGA organization, but in truth the PGA has almost nothing to say about how the tour is run any more.

I don't want to get off on a side track and talk about that old feud, but I supported the PGA all the way. I always wanted to be a PGA pro because I wanted to stay in golf after I was finished playing, running a course or teaching. The PGA isn't much of an organization but it's the only one in the field. I think the Tournament Players Division was a brainchild of people like Gardner Dickinson and Jack Nicklaus and some other amateur politicians who don't want anybody telling them anything about their business. Well, all they created with the TPD is one hell of an expense. I don't see the TPD doing much of anything different, except now the money comes out of our pockets. They said we never saw the money we paid to the PGA—but I never see the money I pay to the TPD. There was a lot of talk about a retirement plan—but no action.

The tour is a $9 million business but it's run like a kids'

lemonade stand. I think every player out here is entitled to a complete accounting of all money spent. We should know the salaries of all the officials, from Beman's $150,000 right on down to the lowliest member of the field staff.

The tour used to be run very nicely with five or six men on the field staff. Now we have eleven or twelve, so one guy can carry coffee over to the other. All we've gained is one hell of an overhead. Jack Tuthill is the head of the field staff. He's a smart man, a former FBI agent; he may have a lot of guts, and he works very long hours, but he doesn't know how to tell people how to do things. The field staff has always been about as well organized as a Fourth of July picnic. If you need a ruling, it takes forever to get it, which doesn't mean you'll understand it. In a war I'd like to have the field staff leading me into battle—I'd never get shot at.

For the most part, the field staff is made up of a bunch of guys who don't know golf. Some of them know the rules, but they don't know or understand the human element in the situations that arise out here. I don't know why we never get former tour players on the field staff, men who've been through it and have a feeling for it.

I'd like to see the field staff get as tough on the top players as it gets with the young players. If a two-stroke penalty for slow play is given out, you can bet it isn't going to go to Nicklaus. There's no consistency in the rulings.

Slow play can choke the tour to death if more isn't done. Some of these players are unbelievable. Bruce Crampton moves like a 95-year-old woman. Bobby Nichols is a sweet man but he can never make up his mind on a club. He wears out six sets of grips a year. For an iron shot to the green, he's got to go to the bag four times. The young players are the slowest, though. Grier Jones gives you the shuffling feet. Jim Simons is a real snail. How those guys get out of bed in the morning is beyond me. It must take them five hours to get dressed. I'd hate to have to watch them choose a pair of socks.

We should be able to play any golf course in four hours,

tops. If a group falls more than a hole behind, there ought to be a two-stroke penalty for everybody in the group. I have the option of breaking away from a slow group, you know. I'm not married to the other two. If I get paired with one of these molasses types, I have the option of going off and leaving him, and I just might do it one of these days.

Since I'm paying for the field staff—and for Beman's fancy offices in Washington near his home—I think I should have more say about how my money is spent. All I get is a vote on the four players who are on the Tournament Policy Board along with three businessmen, three PGA officers, and Beman. I can't write in any candidates. The committee nominates its own successors, so what you get is a big turnover of friends, a buddy system. Dale Douglass put his pal Hale Irwin on the ballot once when Irwin wasn't even eligible to be nominated because he wasn't a full PGA member!

The players who get on the committee all of a sudden know a lot more than they used to. It's amazing how smart a man can get overnight. Jim Colbert is a classic recent example. One day he's one of the boys, the next he's telling me I owe it to golf to play in a designated tournament. Owe it to golf my rear end.

I think we ought to have regular player meetings—of all the players—and anybody who doesn't show is fined. Then the players would have to take an interest in their business and the committee would be accountable to the players.

Given time to assert himself, I have hopes that Beman will become a strong commissioner and straighten out some of these weaknesses in our operation. Unlike Joe Dey, he comes out on the tour quite a bit and listens to our gripes. Joe was good for the time. He took the job in the middle of the turmoil between the players and the PGA and settled things down. He gave us at least the appearance of being a good business because he had such a tremendous reputation for honesty and dedication to golf. He got us on some better courses. He laid the groundwork.

Beman is a good businessman—he made a lot of money in

life insurance when he was younger—and he'll really try to take it from there. He knows we have to do more to help the sponsors promote their tournaments. He knows the telecasts need improving, especially the announcing. He appointed Steve Reid, a friend of his when they were playing the tour, as a television liaison man, which made about as much sense as appointing my teenage son, since Reid had no experience in television. But Reid has worked hard and learned a lot and the telecasts are improving. Some of the players who have done announcing—for free—have told the viewer much more about what's going on.

I notice Beman is dressing better. He's gone from buckskin jackets to $200 Madison Avenue suits. That's fine. I just hope he develops into a commissioner like Pete Rozelle in football, because at this stage of our growth, we badly need one.

Deane was a player, so he can talk our language. His knowing the players is both a disadvantage and an advantage. He can't favor his old friends, but on the other hand he understands how the tour works and what makes players tick.

It would surprise most fans to learn that golf pros are basically very conservative people, about almost everything. Most of us don't follow politics, but if we did we'd be on the far right, somewhere the other side of Goldwater. Beman said it very well one night over a beer in a Florida bar not long after he took the commissioner's job. He said: "Golfers are conservatives because they have a real sense of value about working at a profession and getting back what you put into it. There are no shortcuts in golf. It's a dead honest game. You're entirely self-sufficient. You don't rely on anybody but yourself. You have to police yourself. There's no fudging the way there is in football or basketball where a player tries to grab an opponent's shirt to slow him down. Golfers have a great advantage over the average guy. They can measure their day's work with a score. You can't kid yourself. You have to have the ability to accept failure, whether you're an unknown rookie or

Jack Nicklaus. For all the bright clothes, golfers are very down-to-earth people."

Beman made another point. He said, "There are no specialists on the tour. You have to be able to do it all." That's an interesting remark coming from Deane, because I thought when he was playing the tour he was the best with all fourteen clubs in the bag. He was a little man and he couldn't hit it as far as a lot of 15-handicappers, but he could get closer to the flag with a 4-wood than most players can with a 6-iron.

Beman had a lot of aggravating injuries late in his career. He could have kept playing but felt he'd proved what he set out to prove when he turned pro at 29. He won tournaments and he wasn't going to have to alibi to his grandchildren that he could have been a winning pro if only he'd joined the tour. Now I think he has a chance to be a strong commissioner.

FINES

Commissioner Beman hasn't fined me yet, not as this book went to press anyway. I thought he might put it to me after I had a little public tiff with the man who runs the Houston Golf Association. I won the tournament, which probably got me off the hook.

That all started when I was misquoted by a Houston sportswriter. Just about every time I talk to the press it comes out wrong. The only reporter who has covered the tour and kept what you said in context was Linc Werden of the *New York Times*—and he's retired now.

Actually I haven't been fined since 1970, when I made my hand mashie shot at the Colonial Tournament in Fort Worth. That's the incident that led to my $3 million suit against the Tournament Players Division. The public doesn't know to this day what happened in that legal action, and I'd like to tell you now.

My disgust was with the field staff basically, and it got very

18

heavy early that year at Palm Springs. As you might guess, there are palm trees in Palm Springs. During the Bob Hope Tournament I hit a ball into one of them. The point was that I identified my ball in the tree, which is all that the rules require, and I had about eight witnesses who agreed it was my ball. I took an unplayable lie and the one-stroke penalty, dropped another ball, and played on. I was disqualified because I hadn't put a special mark on my ball, which the rules nowhere call for. There wasn't even an official on the scene!

That had been bugging at me all year. In effect, the field staff had called me a liar. I may be a lot of unprintable names, but a liar isn't one of them. I felt that sooner or later I was going to have to take a stand. I didn't exactly plan to take it in Fort Worth, but that's where things came to a boil.

I never play well in Fort Worth, and on the first day I played like my Aunt Mabel and shot a 79. Back then, before I filed my suit, you had to lie to withdraw from a tournament—had to say you were sick or something. Joe Dey wanted you to show a doctor's certificate as proof you were sick; we were right back in high school. So I don't have a chance to finish well and all I'm doing is getting in the way of my playing partners, but I can't quit. Hell, the way I was hitting it, I could have hurt somebody.

The second day I was playing worse. Pretty soon I was 16 over par and going for the high 80s and just figuring ways to keep from blowing my cool completely. Finally, I topped a drive and decided I'd play the last few holes with one club, a 9-iron. On the eighteenth, a long and tough par-4, I popped three 9 irons and was in the bunker to the right of the green. The ball was buried, out of sight. I thought to myself, "To hell with this."

I did something then I've always thought about doing in a tournament to shake everybody up. I picked the ball out of the sand with my hand and dropped it onto the green. I sort of let it roll off my hand with a little overspin so it would run down toward the hole. I didn't throw it. I had a nice touch on it actually—it finished about two feet from the hole. A helluva hand mashie. I tapped it in with the 9-iron.

I walked over to the scoreboard and told the officials that I was disqualified because I'd made an illegal drop. Jack Tuthill later said I'd signed an incorrect scorecard, but I'd made an illegal drop first. Adios, Fort Worth.

The following week I went on to the tournament at Memphis, where I was defending champion. The TPD accepted my $50 entry fee. Two days after I left Fort Worth I got word over the phone from one of Tuthill's assistants that I'd been fined $500 for "conduct unbecoming a professional golfer." Now Joe Dey could have fined me $500 and all I'd have done was appeal it. But Dey was out of the country, watching the Walker Cup Matches or something. When one of Tuthill's assistants lays it on me without so much as putting it in writing, somebody's going to have to pay the piccolo player. Tuthill didn't have the authority to fine me that way. He does now, since my court case. He didn't then. I didn't get any kind of hearing, no chance to state my case. That was in violation of all our procedures, of any legal procedures in a democratic society.

They got my $500. They also got a fat lawsuit.

I was at a party in Memphis (there's always a party in Memphis during tournament week) and there I met Johnny Colton and the late Jim Irwin of the legal firm of Irwin, Owens, Gillock, Colton & Lyne. They represented a Mr. Tanner, who was throwing the party. Mr. Tanner—Pepper Tanner—has a big company that makes a lot of the singing commercials you see on television. I told Jim and Johnny about the $500 fine and what had happened in the past and they said I had good grounds for a legal action. They weren't looking for business because they had all they could handle. They just wanted to help me, and so I sat down with them the next day and we decided to file suit charging basically that my civil rights and right to free speech were being violated. It was a federal antitrust action.

The TPD policy board responded in a meeting the following week by putting me on a year's probation. I wasn't invited. That ruling didn't mean anything: I could still play and keep my winnings. But it made me madder still. Now I was determined to make the suit stick.

It dragged on for many months. I won't deny it was hurting my play and my temperament. I'm edgy under the best of circumstances, and I was getting worse than a grizzly in heat. Also I was spending a lot of money in legal fees, about $12,000 all told. We finally settled out of court.

I really think I could have won the suit. Lawyers who ought to know tell me that the TPD is a monopoly, vulnerable to that kind of suit. But I didn't want it on my mind any more. I'm a golfer, not a political rabble-rouser. I figured I got concessions on eleven points from the TPD and those were worth what they cost me.

Those points never have been made public. The highlights were that the TPD would come up with a uniform system of fines and penalties for infractions with uniform enforcement, and would work up a system for educating and testing TPD members and officials who run the tour, make rulings, and levy fines.

I never had it in mind to wreck the TPD; carrying the suit through might have done that. All I wanted to do was force a system of equal treatment of all players, especially the young guys. I was fighting for a principle. I think we're gaining on it as a result of the suit.

I certainly wasn't suggesting that we don't need rules. I just want to see the rules administered uniformly, for Arnold Palmer as well as for Joe Jones. There are offenses that call for fines. Profanity is one. Throwing clubs is another. You can kill somebody throwing a golf club in anger. I've only let one club get away from me, several years ago. I slammed it into the ground after a bad shot and it bounced into the air and fell across a woman's lap. She wasn't hurt—but it scared hell out of me. I never threw another club.

I remember Tommy Bolt used to get fined every time he looked like he was going to throw a club. That's fine, except I've seen Arnold Palmer and fellows like that throw clubs —and nobody says a word. Tommy used to make fun of Palmer over his club-throwing form. "That's how smart Palmer is, he throws the club backwards," Tommy would sneer. "You gotta throw it forward, so you can pick it up on your way."

We have had no consistency in our rulings. I was playing one week with Gardner Dickinson, who's been on the tournament committee. He'll help the young players with their swings if they ask, but he doesn't smile too much. He hit an iron shot into a bunker once and slammed the club down and buried it in the ground. Gardner never gets fined, though. But I'm not a policeman. I'm not going to run over to an official and say, "Look! Look! He buried the club in the ground!" I have buried a few in the ground, you know. It took two men to get one of them out. All I was saying in that suit is that what's fair for one is fair for all. I'm still saying it.

Jack Nicklaus came out one year and said to newspapermen in Hawaii that he wasn't going to play in the tournament again. He said something negative about the golf course or the wind or whatever, and it was all over the papers. I get crucified for cracks like that, but is Jack Nicklaus fined?

I firmly believe there is prejudice in applying the rules and regulations of the tour and fining people. The rules aren't the same for Dave Hill or Ray Floyd as they are for Jack Nicklaus or Arnold Palmer. If you're a big name, you're protected when you have a little temper tantrum.

When Mike Souchak was on the tour, he pulled a stunt one time that cost him $100 but probably would have cost me ten times that much. We were playing together in Phoenix, on the eighteenth green, and he had a putt for a 67. He missed it and kicked his putter, and as I was walking up to address my own putt his putter hit me in the left hand and then traveled another 35 or 40 feet into the gallery. If it hadn't caught me a glancing blow on the thumb it would have broken my hand. He'd endangered my livelihood and the health of the gallery and for that he was fined all of $100.

As bad as some people think my disposition is, I've never done anything that could hurt anybody but myself—never. I've broken a lot of clubs, but I've broken them over my own knee or wrapped them, literally, around my own neck. One day I was so hot after a round I went around the corner where nobody could see me and I broke every club in my bag. I felt better.

Also, if I break a law I don't try to get away with anything. I'll turn myself in and pay the penalty. I'm a big law and order man. I know the rules and regulations and I don't try to give anybody a fast shuffle. My philosophy is that if you don't like the rules, you should campaign to get them changed. In the meantime, you're obliged to live by them, whether you're on the golf tour or driving your car down the street. Break a rule and you should expect to pay for it.

I've joked that I keep a separate bank account for my tour fines. To tell you the truth, I don't know how much I've been fined over the years. I'm sure I'm up there with the league leaders. I think Bob Rosburg and Tommy Bolt have an edge on me in breaking clubs, but they're no longer active players.

I had a good year in 1961. I paid something like $1,400 in fines, most of them for breaking putters. It cost me $100 per broken club. I really don't see why I shouldn't be allowed to break a piece of my own equipment if the spirit moves me. I really don't see why I shouldn't be allowed to jump out of a fifth-story window if the spirit moves me. That's what I want to do and I'm not hurting anybody but myself.

23

My first major run-in with the tour committee was in 1963. My father had died early that year and I wasn't in a good frame of mind in general. At the Frank Sinatra Tournament I had a chance to win but ran into a bad case of the 3-putts. I was burning up inside but I held my temper until the eighteenth green. I had about a 15-foot birdie putt. I casually walked over to Joe Black, a gangling Texan who was the tour director at the time, and said, "Joe, if I miss this one, I think I'm going to break this putter." He said, "Oh, you don't want to do that." And I said, "I just promised myself I would."

I missed the putt and I broke the putter over my knee, into two pieces. I had one piece in one hand and the other piece in the other hand, and I tapped the ball in with the piece that had the head on it.

I left the tour to get some teeth capped, and the committee had a meeting and suspended me for two months, a major penalty under the PGA's constitution. The constitution further stated that a player is to be notified if he is up for a major penalty. He could be present at the meeting. I was suspended with no notice of anything. I took it lying down, but I made up my mind I wouldn't take it that way again. You can commit murder in this country and still have your day in court. I didn't object to the penalty—I objected to the way it was handed down without a hearing of any kind.

On the committee then were players Bob Goalby, who called and gave me the word of my suspension, Dave Marr, and Jay Hebert. I later heard that Marr wanted to ban me for a year and had Hebert ready to go along with him, but Joe Black and Goalby fought and got it down to two months. Apparently the fact that I broke the club on television made it a worse offense to some.

I have always said one player should have nothing to do with judging another. That structure has to cause hard feelings. We have some great clubhouse lawyers out here, and if you give them a whiff of power they start acting like Hitler. It's a bad system.

GAMBLING

You hear a lot about gambling in golf. Here's the way it really is. When the Tournament of Champions was held in Las Vegas, before it moved to La Costa in California, it drew a lot of betting action. People could bet one player against his playing partner for the day, for example. One day I was paired with Arnold Palmer and he was favored over me by a stroke and a half at even money—if you wanted me without any stroke advantage you got odds of something like 9 to 5. I knew that Phil Harris, the comedian, had bet several thousand dollars on me and taken the stroke and a half.

Palmer led me by a shot coming to the last hole. Phil had been following us the entire round and was looking extremely hopeful. On his bet I was ahead. There was water on the right of the fairway and when Palmer hit his drive into that water Phil beamed like a man who had just inherited a small fortune. He figured he had.

I should have been thinking more about my drive and less about Phil's bet. I set up aiming so far left I didn't think I could possibly hit it into the water on the right. I put a woodchopper's swing on it, neck-sliced it, and the ball ran over into the water. I measured off two club lengths from the lateral hazard and made my drop—and the ball rolled under a bush. I spent five minutes trying to determine that the ball rolled more than two club lengths so I could redrop it, but I couldn't.

I had to play the ball from under the bush. I wriggled into the bush, contorting myself and ruining my slacks, and finally addressed it—and the damn thing moved! I had to add a penalty stroke for that. To make a painful story short, I had an 8 on the hole and lost to Palmer on Phil's bet. If he hadn't come out to watch me, I'm sure I wouldn't have made worse than 5 or 6 on the hole, but I was trying so hard to beat Arnold so Phil could win his bet, I couldn't play. Phil and I have been good friends for a long time and he took it better than I did, although I don't remember him saying anything funny.

I know the bookmakers out there to this day think I went in the tank—threw the match because I had money on Palmer. I didn't, but I'll have to admit it looked bad. That's the trouble with playing a tournament in Vegas. The Calcutta for the Tournament of Champions, where you would bid for a player, used to be worth several times more money than first prize, and there was no telling what would happen. Golfers as a group are more honest than any other I know, but there's no sense inviting temptation. The Vegas booking places eventually limited a bet on a player to $500, but you could bet about as much as you wanted to with a gambler head up. It wasn't hard to find action.

The Tournament of Champions today is run by the same people who ran it in Vegas, but changing the locale stopped most of the worry that the tournament could be fixed. Some of those people reputedly have underworld ties and use the spa at La Costa as a super-comfortable retreat, but that's just hearsay as far as I'm concerned. I've never seen anything irregular. The pros don't look far past the golf course and the hospitality, which is sensational. Everything at the plush resort is complimentary for players and their wives.

If a fellow really wants to get a bet down at a golf tournament, it wouldn't be that difficult. In Britain they've experimented with betting shops at the course, and all the racing bookies take golf bets. Around country clubs in America you have to look harder, but you can always find people who are looking for the kick of a little extra action. The money isn't big enough to threaten the tour's integrity. Golf has never had a major scandal. That's no reason to presume it never will have one, but as the purses get bigger, the chances get more remote.

When I first came out on the tour the prize money was so small you could make more money betting on yourself than you could winning the tournament. I have bet on myself to beat another guy—not lately, but I have. I guess that makes me as bad as Paul Hornung and Alex Karras, who were suspended from pro football for betting on their teams—me and a few hundred other pro athletes. Several years ago Al Besselink was put on probation for betting on himself. He said at the time that trying to legislate gambling out of golf was like trying to outlaw breathing, and he's correct. But today you don't feel the urge to bet. You have too much at stake in prize money. If people even suspect that the tour is tainted, we lose big.

That's why I was alarmed when I found out that a player out here—a pretty good player who has won a few tournaments—has been betting big amounts of money in strange ways during tournaments. I haven't called him on it because I want to be completely sure of my facts, but I believe he paid another player $3,000 to shoot at least 77 on a recent Sunday. The player who took the money was out of contention, but it's still bad. The player doing the betting showed me a sheet and it had about fifteen names on it. Let's say he was betting on me to beat ten of those players for the tournament. I'm a virtual cinch after three rounds to beat nine of them, and he pays the tenth guy to shoot at least 77 and in effect lose to me.

The same player was sniffing at another tournament, asking me if I thought I could beat Frank Beard. I gave him an innocuous answer, told him I was playing pretty well and Frank hadn't been sharp lately. Maybe that's all he wanted to hear. He could have had something bet on me against Frank.

This kind of thing is dangerous for our image, and if the player is guilty, he has to be punished and held up as an example. I'm confident he'll be trapped. I don't know who he's betting with; I imagine it's somebody not connected with the tour. He's never offered me money to shoot a high score and I hope he never does, because I might immediately put that many strokes on the side of his head with a driver.

I'm not pure. I figure everyone has his price—it's just that mine isn't $3,000. I was offered $2,500 by a gambler in Vegas once to be sure I didn't beat a certain player, and I told the man if he'd like to multiply his offer by ten, I would consider it. Now my price would have to be considerably higher, high enough so I could afford to live luxuriously ever after if I got caught and could never play the tour again. Say three-quarters of a million. That's my going rate to be fixed. Give me a collect call if you're interested.

Nobody is going to bet that kind of money on a golf tournament. That's why no good player will be prone to fix a tournament. If he weren't scrupulously honest, which he is, how much money do you think it would take to buy off a Jack Nicklaus? A million? Two million? Five million? Hell, the man's making damn near that much every year with his off-course income on top of his winnings. How much could a gambler bet and still fix the tournament? It isn't believable with today's purses as big as they are.

Besides, I don't think there's enough bad money in the world to offer a golfer who has a chance to win. Oh, I could conceive of a situation where a man has a chance to win his first tournament and he's playing with you the final day and you're the only one who can beat him. It could be worth it to him to offer you the equivalent of first-place money plus a bonus to let him win. But I've never heard of it happening and I'd be surprised if it ever did. Another far-out possibility is that gamblers could hire a player who is paired with a favorite to use gamesmanship on him and upset him, but it's very unlikely.

I could pick up a pretty good piece of change every week betting with the local club swingers. I'd do it by betting for the final day against the leader. People want to bet on the leader but they don't realize that the leader is not going out there to try to shoot 64 or 65. He's going out there to try to protect his lead. He wants to make a couple of birdies, par everything else and come in with a 70 or 71. That will win most tournaments. If you have a big lead of five or six shots you usually can shoot a little over par and still win. You aren't going to run any unnecessary risks. Going into the green you'll shoot at the middle of the green instead of at the flag the way you did the first three days. Your game plan is to hit every green in regulation and get down in two putts. Two-putt, two-putt, two-putt. It's like getting pecked to death by a duck. If a twenty-foot putt happens to drop, so much the better.

The player who's back in the pack, on the other hand, is anxious to move up and make a good check. He's going to take chances he wouldn't ordinarily take and he's liable to shoot lights out. He's under no heavy pressure and he can relax and shoot at the hole with his approach shots. With that attitude you can get some low numbers.

The condition of the course is another reason you shouldn't bet on the leaders to shoot low scores the last day. The leaders tee off last, when the greens have been trampled on by the entire field. The players who tee off early have at least a two-shot edge because the greens are in better shape.

Most of the pros like to bet in practice rounds. It's against the tour rules to gamble at the course but nobody enforces the ban. If you have money on the line it keeps you trying and thinking and working. Frank Beard has made a lot of young mommas mad by saying it did his career good to start wagering what he had in his jeans pockets when he was a kid, but I know what he means. I feel the same way. If you're betting your own money and you can't really afford to lose, you treat every shot seriously and learn to concentrate under pressure. We have dozens of young players trying the tour every year who have pretty swings but don't know how to hold up under pressure, and they disappear before you can learn their names.

Back in the old days when purses weren't so big, a player wanted to make $100 in practice rounds to get him through the week. Today the top 60 players don't need $100 that badly but you get plenty of action if you want it. A two dollar Nassau is the common bet, but once you complicate it with presses, greenies, and all the other side deals, you easily can be going for $100. Some of the good younger players like to play for a lot of money for the sport of it and sometimes to rub it in to the older guys. Lanny Wadkins, a cocky kid, relieved Arnold Palmer of $800 one day and was chiding Palmer in front of a bunch of people to come back for more. Lanny went to Wake Forest on an Arnold Palmer Scholarship and Arnold didn't like it when he dropped out of school to turn pro, which made the exchange all the more interesting.

It's funny how some players play better when their own money is on the line and some play worse. Jack Nicklaus is the best example of a star who isn't all that keen to play for his own money. He isn't going to fold up, of course, but he definitely doesn't play as well under that kind of pressure as he does when he's playing for somebody else's money in a tournament. He has a lot of company. Some guys get so nervous playing for their own money, the greens don't need fertilizing for a year. Prize money isn't actually yours until the tournament is over, and I never have as great a sense of loss if I miss out on a $30,000 winner's check as if I blow a hundred bucks out of my own pocket.

Sam Snead remains the all-time best practice round player. He plays better in practice rounds than he does in tournaments. For a $20 Nassau that SOB will shoot anything at you—a 61, anything. I don't know if it's because of his legendary closeness with his money or what, but he is the best at playing for his own money I've ever seen.

Doug Ford tells about the time he and Bob Goalby were playing against Snead and Jerry Barber in a practice round at the Masters. Ford and Goalby were ahead after the first six holes and Snead and Barber pressed—added a bet. The last three holes on the front side at Augusta are a tricky 365-yard par-4, an uphill 530-yard par-5, and a dogleg 420-yard par-4, all with sloping greens. Snead finished 3-3-3 to win all bets.

Snead has three tremendous strengths playing for his own money, apart from his super swing. First, he picks his partners and opponents carefully, giving himself every good chance to win. Second, he manages his bets astutely. He knows when to bet and when to keep quiet. If he's going well, he'll increase the bet; if his opponents are hot, he won't. Third, but certainly not least, he is not rattled by gamesmanship and if necessary can give better than he gets. A young pro was playing against Snead in a practice round and tried to shake Sam's concentration by kidding him about his sidesaddle putting style. "Son," snarled Sam, "don't fool with me. I've got a needle longer than your leg." And he does.

Gamesmanship is more common in practice rounds than

during tournaments. In tournaments you're almost always playing against too many other guys to give special attention to shaking up your playing partner. In practice rounds it's head-to-head competition, match play, and different ploys go with that. Some of the older pros who have a greater variety of shots will catch a young pro looking in their bags to see what club they're selecting and lay a trick shot on him, letting up on a 4-iron and fading it softly into a green when they normally would have hit a 6-iron, for instance. If the young pro takes the bait, he'll hit a 4-iron twenty yards over the green.

A popular form of gamesmanship is to slow down a player who likes to play fast or speed up a player who likes to go slow. You'd be surprised how many players have to move at a certain pace or else lose their composure. As a slow player walks casually to his ball, maybe an opponent will say, "We'd better hurry it up. They're waiting on the tee." The slow player is distracted from his shot.

We have a few players out here who will try almost anything to upset another player. One veteran is famous for standing on the tee as you prepare to drive and making tearing sounds with the adjustable stick-on strap on the back of his glove. Another wears gleaming white shoes and makes sure to stand in your field of vision and cross his feet at the wrong time. Another is a notorious grunter when you are over the ball.

Verbal gamesmanship is always the most subtle. A player will grab one of your clubs, sole it thoughtfully, and then remark that he doesn't see how you can play so well with such flat-lying clubs. His objective is to get you thinking about something other than playing your usual game, and if you aren't careful it can work without your knowing it. "Have you always used such a strong grip?" a gamesman might ask you in the middle of a match. If you let an element of doubt about your grip creep into your thinking, you're in trouble, and he knows it.

The best defense against gamesmanship is to ignore it. The gamesman is putting himself at a potential disadvantage because he's letting his own mind wander from his game to yours. If you don't let him bother you, his gamesmanship can work in your favor. If all else fails, violence has been known to work. One outraged player put a needler over his shoulder one afternoon and flung him into a nearby pond. The wet victim didn't resort to gamesmanship again.

Tour players occasionally are gamesmen for gambling reasons but they almost never are hustlers. A hustler is someone who misrepresents his ability to beat opponents out of money. It's not very easy for a pro to lie about his ability. We play matches against each other all even. To be a hustler, you have to be a better player than you appear to be, and you aren't going to fool anybody very long on the tour. You hear a lot of stories about Lee Trevino's hustling background or Doug Sanders' hustling background, but you never know how much of that stuff to believe. Those two guys *could* have been great hustlers because at first glance you don't think they can play nearly as well as they can.

I've heard that Trevino used to play in a lot of big money matches before he came on the tour, but I imagine someone else was making the matches and putting up the dough and he was just playing for a small percentage of the winnings. Ten percent or so. There's a generally accepted story that Lee and his friends early on took a prominent tour player for $25,000 in two weeks. The tour stud thought he had stumbled across easy pickings, got in the hole, and didn't know when to quit, upping the bets in a futile attempt to get out.

George Low, who calls himself the world's greatest putter and probably is, hangs around the tour and has hustled more money on the putting green than most pros have earned in their careers. George used to be a good player—he was the low pro in the Memphis Open the year amateur Freddie Haas ended Byron Nelson's record winning streak—but he prefers the easy life. He's in his sixties now and doesn't do much besides represent a company that manufactures putters with his name on them, give putting lessons, and give famous people the honor of his entertaining presence as a house guest. Jimmy Demaret says George was born retired. George himself has a line for every occasion. Listening to a pro run off at the mouth after a bad round, he turned to a bystander and snapped, "Put a head cover over his head."

George has patented gimmicks to take the money of unsuspecting suckers in putting matches. He will bet you that he can out-putt you with the side of his foot. He can, largely because he has practiced putting with his foot and has had his shoes especially made with an instep like a putter blade. He has rigged umbrellas to work like putters. He can putt better with a wedge than most people can with a putter. Low reportedly was driving Frank Stranahan's big car across the country once—and he lost it in a crap game. Stranahan said he didn't mind losing the car as much as the fancy wardrobe that was in it.

When hustling stories are being swapped, the late Titanic Thompson's name is always up front. He was a good player in the Snead-Nelson-Hogan era but, like Low, he built his fame and fortune off the tour or in its shadows. His imagination was wild. He bet a big, strong man that the man couldn't carry two bricks for two miles and set them up on a counter in a hotel. The man had no trouble carrying the bricks into the hotel, but when he raised his arms to set them up on the tall counter, his hands inevitably opened and he dropped the bricks.

Another time Thompson was sitting in a chair on the porch of a hotel with a rich companion. A crippled old man hobbled past on the street. A young man was walking rapidly behind him about to overtake him. Thompson turned to his rich companion and said, "I'll bet you $5,000 the old man beats the kid to the corner." It was only 50 yards to the corner and the kid was moving out. The rich companion leaped to take the bet. But just before the young man got to the corner, he turned and went into a building. Thompson collected. He had been sitting on the hotel porch three straight days and had seen the young man turn into that building every day to go to work.

Thompson once bet a guy he could drive a golf ball a mile—and won the bet by driving off the top of a mountain. He was walking around Houston one day with a group of people, eating a sack of peanuts, and he bet them he could throw a peanut over a three-story building. He picked one out of the sack and heaved it over the building. The one peanut he picked was loaded with lead.

Sometimes the hustlers get hustled. A young pro in Atlanta got a call from a friend who told him there was a lot of money to be hustled from a couple of wealthy movie stars he knew. They drove to California, hustling along the way, and plotted their strategy. When they got there and practiced, the young pro was to stay under wraps and hit nothing longer than a 5-iron. The kid was a good player and when he practiced out there he drew a few people who complimented his swing. He responded by working up to hitting booming driver shots. One of the movie stars was watching from the clubhouse and suspected a fishy deal.

When the kid stopped practicing, the movie star introduced himself and invited him to stay in his guest house. When the kid arrived there, he found his host and three beautiful actresses. The movie star told him to enjoy everything in the guest house and left the kid with the three girls. Tee time the next morning was at nine o'clock, and the kid showed up an hour late looking wiped out; he shot a smooth 88 to cost his partner somewhere around $25,000. The movie star who saw through the hustle was Bob Hope and his partner was Bing Crosby.

The big hustlers these days are amateur golfers, not pros. The pros have those big purses to keep them off the streets. A real hustler is a guy who tells you he has an 8 handicap and then plays to a 3. And it's amazing how many people in the world almost walk around looking to be hustled. Bobby Riggs says that when he was hustling golf, he never had to lie about his handicap, he just let his opponents talk themselves into a trap.

Millions of golfers pretend to have lower handicaps than they can play to, for ego reasons. I see it in my pro-am partners week after week. I've had very few partners who played to their handicaps. One reason is they are apt to be playing on a strange course and one that's tougher than the familiar little track where they built their handicaps. They're fine people, most of them, and intelligent until they start talking about their handicaps.

Joe Louis lost thousands every year playing with a handicap that was too low. Say a man has been an 8-handicapper for ten years but recently he shot a couple of rounds in the high 70s, so he announces he's a 5. That sounds good, but as soon as he faces pressure, he's going to shoot way over his old handicap, let alone his contrived new one. If you bet him enough money, he won't be able to break 85. I've seen golfers like this really come apart and shoot over 90 when they accept a hustler's challenge to shoot, say, an 85, a score that seems within reasonable reach. That's suicide.

I enjoy playing with amateurs for money, giving them plenty of strokes. I do it often at home in Denver at the little municipal course a friend and I lease from the city for fun. The tour is too wearing, and my favorite getaway spot is the Canyon Hotel and Country Club in Palm Springs. There are some great people who go there to relax and get a little action, not necessarily in that order. One gentleman brings a hundred thousand dollars to gamble each winter and stays until it's gone. I've seen condominiums change hands in the course of 18 holes. I avoid some of the big games. I have a regular circle of friends I play with there and I give them as many strokes as they think they have to have to play me, then we renegotiate during the round if it isn't working out. Nobody tries to hustle anybody, not maliciously at least. Gambling makes the game more enjoyable if you gamble sensibly.

CHEATING

Golf is the hardest game in the world to play and the easiest to cheat at. You don't see as much fudging on the tour as you do in the average weekend Nassau match, but cheating is a problem among the pros. That ball is awfully small, the players are scattered out with no referees, and it isn't that hard to get away with breaking the rules.

I'd guess that only about one percent of the tour players cheat with any regularity. Four or five players a week are taking advantage of everybody else—and threatening all our reputations with the public watching. Usually the guys who cheat are older players who have trouble scoring as well as they did when they were younger, or players who aren't sure of their ability to compete against the best. There are a couple of exceptions, prominent players. One player high on the list of all-time money winners has cheated for years. He's been so blatant about it that most of us who have been around for a while joke about him. I always say he's advanced the ball farther illegally than Jimmy Brown has carried it for the Cleveland Browns.

Most cheating takes place on the greens. The guy who stuffs his coin up under the ball when he marks it is the guy I watch. He's going to sneak an inch or two when he puts the ball back down to putt. We're supposed to mark the ball by placing a small coin behind the ball directly in line with the hole. The coin isn't supposed to touch the ball: you leave a quarter of an inch. If you jam the coin up under the ball, you're going to have trouble getting it out from under the ball when you replace it.

The way I look at it, the inch or two the guy can gain toward the hole isn't enough to help him. But where he can get an edge is if his ball was in a hole and he marks it and replaces it to the side of the coin so that the ball no longer is in the hole. It's tricky putting a ball out of a hole. It's even easier to sneak your ball out of a hole if your ball is in another player's line and you follow the accepted procedure and move your coin two clubheads one way or the other. The proper way to move it is to place the putter by the coin, move the coin to the other end of the putter and pull the putter back over the coin and move the coin again. But you will see players put the putter down and just move it two clubheads and then put the coin down. You can change the position of your ball an inch that way.

People cheat in every business. But golfers are on display where their indiscretions can be noticed by millions.

The worst case of cheating on the greens probably was several years ago on the Caribbean Tour. An American player was moving his ball six and eight and ten feet at a whack. You would think that's too preposterous to get away with, and eventually it was, but it isn't that simple to catch a cheater. The players in a group often come up to a green from different directions. You know yourself you will hit an iron shot to a green and think the ball is 60 feet from the hole, but when you get to the green it's more like six feet, or vice versa.

Well, this player would hurry to be the first one on the green. He had a long Ping putter and he would scoop the ball up on the back of the putterhead as he bent over and tossed a coin down, and by the time his playing partners were on the green he was putting last instead of first. Inevitably he got caught—and all he got was a three-month suspension! He also had to take psychiatric treatment. It was a sickness with him, like kleptomania. Instead of going into a department store and feeling a compulsion to stuff something in his pocket and leave without paying for it, he felt a compulsion to move his ball on the green. He somehow has managed to hold down a good club job in the Northeast and still comes out on the tour once in a while. I haven't seen him enough to know whether he's cured or not.

More recently a great furor was raised over the case of Janie Blalock, the lady pro who was suspended and then went into a series of bitter lawsuits with her association and fellow players. Her case, which finally was settled in her favor, came closer than most people know to ruining the ladies' tour. I don't know whether she was guilty or innocent. Actually the court squabbles had nothing to do with her guilt or innocence, but were based on the question of whether a player can be suspended by a board of fellow competitors who stand to gain from her absence. I sent her an encouraging note because I know what it's like to buck the establishment and I think she went through a ton of hell and was assumed guilty with no regard for due legal process. How she continued to play well under that kind of pressure, I don't know. The fact that she did makes me guess she was innocent, because she didn't need to cheat to be a champion. Unless she was the victim of an illness like the fellow we just talked about.

Actually you could trap almost anybody on the greens. Many honest players cheat unintentionally. I'm sure I do once in a while. It can be very difficult to put the ball back in its original position after you've marked it. You may think you've placed the coin dead behind the ball, but when you put it back down, the ball rolls slightly to the right. Well, that must have been where it was, because it settles to the lowest point on the green. Or the ball will roll over as a player tries to respot it. He tries to get it back in front of the coin but he easily could be a half inch off. Or he approaches his coin from a different angle than when he marked the ball and misspots the ball. That kind of thing is not done on purpose and I wouldn't call it cheating. But if you were looking to trap someone you could call it cheating.

Some people believe a golfer should never be allowed to touch his ball anywhere on the course. I agree up to a point. You have to let a man clean his ball on the green, though; otherwise the playing conditions can change for one man and not for another. The man who flies the ball into a soft green with a lot of backspin on the shot might get a ball that has a big clump of mud on it and is almost impossible to putt. The golfer who runs the ball onto that green, on the other hand, will have a clean ball. Also, if you have a morning tee time, you're going to be playing on greens messy with dew, and if you can't clean your ball you're at a disadvantage against the player who plays later in the day. I don't see why a player needs to clean his ball more than once, though, after it lands on the green. After that, leave it alone until it's in the hole.

There is also considerable disagreement over how much you should be able to touch the line of your putt. You can remove loose impediments, of course, which is fine and seldom causes any misunderstanding. But you cannot repair cleat marks made by a player who doesn't walk as carefully as he should. Ball marks yes; cleat marks no. I've even known a couple of players who would deliberately put cleat marks in the path of your putt if they thought they could get away with it. Again, we're talking about a tiny percentage of the players—most of them are as honest as Superman—but cleat marks can affect a putt whether they're made by design or accident. Lee Trevino has always recommended that a player should be able to repair all the scars on his putting line, including cleat marks. The party line is that ball marks are easier to define than cleat marks and a player could brush a path all the way to the hole under the pretense of cleaning up cleat marks, heaven forbid. I'll accept that, but I'll say that some players have an uncommonly hard time distinguishing between ball marks and cleat marks.

As I say, most of the cheating that exists on the tour takes place on the greens and is pretty subtle. But you do find cheating elsewhere on the course, and although there's less of it there, it's more glaring and costly. I haven't seen or heard of anybody moving the ball to a better lie in the rough for several years, but it has happened. One older player who isn't out here any more used to do it as big as you please. I won't say who he is, because that wouldn't do anybody any good. He'd just take his clubhead and shove the ball into a better position. I was standing on the tee one day with George Bayer and Jay Hebert. We were held up and I was watching the group behind us play up on a par-5. This fellow was short of the green in long tall grass in two strokes. I was only about 40 yards away but couldn't see the ball at all, it was so far down in the rough. I looked away as he arrived at his ball, and when I looked back, lo and behold, he was addressing the ball and I could see it sitting up like a big balloon.

It's hard as hell for anybody to get out of that kind of trash, so when a guy cheats, he's possibly picking up a full shot on the field. This particular player had a reputation as one of the fastest players on the tour and I think I know why. He walked fast so he could get up there and put some cute moves on his ball in the rough. It wasn't as bad as it might have been, because this player was well past his prime and couldn't have beaten a good player with a free shot every third hole. He apparently couldn't adjust to not playing as well as he had played in his good years, and he resorted to cheating. It was sad really.

Another dishonest method for improving your lie in the

41

rough is to address the ball and press down with the clubhead behind it. It's possible, too, to walk to your ball as you "find" it and press down the high grass behind it with your feet.

Violations in the fairway usually come when we're permitted to move the ball because the ground is designated as under repair for one reason or another, maybe because of recent heavy rains. Naturally, a handful of guys take illegal advantage. When you're allowed to move the ball one club length to a better lie, it's only good common sense to measure that club length with your driver, because it's your longest club. But I watched a fellow the other day who was measuring with his driver and not taking the head cover off! It was one of those big fancy knit head covers, and damned if he wasn't grabbing an extra three inches to get an even better lie. I mean, if there isn't anywhere to tee it up within a club length on the fairway, there isn't anyplace to tee it up period.

Some guys will move the ball more than a club length and still not be content. They have to fashion themselves a little tee to take further advantage of the situation. There are several ways a clever player can get away with this. He'll step hard with his foot and leave an impression to one side of the ball, then when he moves the ball, he'll nudge it up to the top of that impression so it sits up a quarter inch to a half inch. It is illegal to step down behind your ball to improve your lie and it is just as illegal to do it to one side of the ball. The officials are already letting you improve your lie by moving your ball a club length, but they're not letting you tee it up, for chrissake. Another way is to scrape around with your hands if you're being allowed to place the ball by hand. You can rough up the grass until you have yourself a tee as workable as any wooden tee you ever saw.

Teeing up the ball illegally can make a lot of difference in a tournament. You see guys hitting drivers off the fairway for their second shots on par-5 holes and reaching the green, whereas they couldn't have reached the green if they'd played fair and hit a 3-wood or long iron out of a worse lie. Not everybody can play a shot with a fairway wood or long iron when the ball's down in a hole or divot. It takes skill to bring off a shot like that. It's damn hard to get the ball up. If you have one or two guys teeing it up high, that hurts everybody else.

The same is true around the greens. If you miss a green and have to pitch the ball from a tight lie, you always have to worry about catching the ball thin and sculling it or chili-dipping it short. But if you can jack it around and get the ball teed up, it's pretty easy to make a good pitch. Again, we're talking about the exception and not the rule when we talk about cheating, but when it can mean a quick shift of two or three strokes, it's a crucial matter. It makes it tough for the best player to win.

You can eliminate the problem by never allowing anybody to touch the ball from tee to green. That's how the game was intended to be played; this business of moving the ball all over the place is an unfortunate modern trend. A lot of fans who watch our tournaments on television don't like it and I don't blame them. Many weekend players abide strictly by the rules and as a result they're playing a tougher golf course; they justifiably see no reason why the big-shot pros should be taking the easy way out. The people who really scream are the club members at tournament sites. They don't like to see their respectable course demeaned by a dozen 65s every day because the pros are moving the ball. Tee it up and Agatha Fagworthy can break par.

Why don't we play the ball where we find it? If it's in a footprint or soft spot or gopher hole, that's the rub of the green. It has been since the Scots popularized the game several centuries ago. Old Tom Morris must spin in his grave when he sees us moving the ball several feet to get an easy lie. He'd say golf was never meant to be a fair game. If you get a bad break today, you'll probably get a good one tomorrow. Everybody gets "unfair" breaks in golf. That's one reason it's the most challenging and intriguing game there is. Play the ball as it lies, and if you touch it you're socked with a two-stroke penalty. Then we'd cut down cheating. We'd also speed up play in a game getting dangerously slow. There'd be no need for all these silly rules interpretations with a player holding up the whole field for twenty minutes waiting for an official to come out from the clubhouse and tell him if he's entitled to a free drop. The answer should be no.

All these rules interpretations leave me cold anyway. The average weekend golfer doesn't know the rules but assumes the average touring pro does. The average touring pro is probably as ignorant as the duffer. He doesn't bother to learn the rules because he knows he can always call for an official to make a ruling. (The larger problem is that the rules, written by the amateur governing bodies of this country and Great Britain and not the pros, are phrased in language that nobody can understand, with dozens of unnecessary qualifications.) Knowing that these officials are on the course, the player takes the lazy way out.

It isn't exactly cheating, but I've always felt that some star players get more favorable rulings than the rest of us. I cannot think of a single unfavorable ruling that's been laid on Arnold Palmer over the years. At the Masters one year he left a shot in a sand bunker and hit the sand with his club in disgust. That's plainly a breach of the rules, and Jack Tuthill, a tour official on the scene, told Palmer it was. But Palmer appealed and the tournament committee overturned the decision. Another time at Augusta an official ruled that Palmer's ball wasn't imbedded at the twelfth hole and he had to play it. Palmer played a provisional ball anyway and the committee ruled for him in that case too. And another time I got a two-stroke penalty for using field glasses in a tournament. The ruling was that they constituted an artificial aid. Okay, so the next year Palmer, who was having trouble with his vision, looked through field glasses from the tee down the fairway of the eighteenth hole at Pebble Beach before he hit—and got no penalty! I'm not saying he cheated, I'm saying that when you have all these rules interpretations and exceptions to the basic rules, you leave the door open for inconsistencies and favored treatment for the big names.

The worst case of cheating I've seen on the tour was off the course a couple of years ago in New Orleans. It involved a player deliberately falsifying his scorecard. The guy, who was from Latin America, was either incredibly ballsy or incredibly dumb. This was after the second round, and 145 was going to make the cut. He had shot 146 and was checking his scorecard in the tent. A playing partner keeps your score during the round (remember the infamous incident at the Masters Tournament when Tommy Aaron made a mistake in Roberto de Vicenzo's card and Roberto didn't catch it and lost a tie for the green jacket?). The Latin American changed the score he had made on a hole, from a 5 to a 4. Here's how brilliant the guy was. His playing partner made his figure 4 closed at the top. When this guy changed the 5 to the 4, he made a figure 4 that was open at the top! The Latin American made the cut—but two days later he was caught and quietly suspended and I don't think he's been back on the tour. I don't know how he thought he could get away with something that flagrant. The players on the borderline to make the cut always check the scoreboard closely and know what everybody shot. If I play with you, I know what you shot. Other players turned him in and I think they did the right thing.

If a player is filching a few inches on the greens, I'm not going to say anything. He still has to make the putt, and if he's that hard up he isn't going to beat me anyway. If he can sleep at night, I sure can. I'm going to look at him so he'll know that I know, because embarrassment can be the quickest cure for a cheater, but I'm not going to turn him in.

I'm not going to say anything if the ball moves when a player is addressing it either, which frequently happens. Nine guys

45

out of ten will call the penalty on themselves. A lot of fans don't realize that's a violation and some players don't either. Jack Nicklaus didn't until recently. With Jack it doesn't make much difference because he doesn't ground the club and therefore is never fully at address. I don't sole the club unless it looks as though the ball might move. It's a stupid rule, anyway. If the ball's moving, you have a more difficult shot, and that's penalty enough.

If I see a more obvious violation, I'm going to turn the guy in. I don't want to be a policeman, but if I think a cheater is going to cost me and a lot of other pros a fair chance at winning money, I owe it to the tour to report him. Then if the officials don't want to do anything about it, I've done all I am going to do. Bruce Crampton is disliked by many pros because he's strict about the rules and isn't bashful about calling infractions. Bruce goes further than I do. For one thing, he's one of only about a half dozen guys out here who really know the rules; also, he was brought up to be rigidly honest by a father who was a policeman, and that's the only way Bruce knows how to be. He feels very strongly that we have to protect our image with the fans as complete professionals, and that if we're seen cheating, even in some petty way, we're jeopardizing our very existence. I have to admire him for that attitude.

One player out here never gets reported for cheating because he's a strong, strapping guy who would just as soon knock your head off as look at you. I've seen him stuff a couple of people into lockers because he didn't like something they said. He'll try anything—I've even heard he uses green tees in the rough. But nobody has the guts to report him. Fortunately he can't play well enough to beat anybody. He couldn't hit a bull in the ass with a spade from three paces.

Golf is still played mainly on the honor system and, quaint as that sounds, it almost always works. In no other sport are the competitors responsible for their scores. The one percent of the golfers who cheat more than an occasional nudge of the ball on the green don't really damage the essential integrity of the game. Despite the unparalleled frustrations and temptations, most players never cheat a bit—they bend over backward to call penalties on themselves if there's the slightest chance they broke the rules. I see less cheating in golf than in any other sport, I'm proud to say.

CADDIES

Golf tournaments aren't held in public arenas like other sports. For the most part, we play at exclusive country clubs and resorts. As long as I've been on the tour, I have never felt comfortable in this atmosphere. When I've had a stomachful of people putting on airs and talking about their status symbols—their big boats and parties and trips to the hottest new island retreat—I have a sure way to relax and get back to reality. I go and spend some time with the tour caddies.

I know it shocks other players that I enjoy having a few drinks or a few rolls of the dice with the caddies. But they talk my language. They're strong individualists and a lot of laughs. They have their own jive language like musicians, and they can tell funny stories about their travels so you never want to go to bed. I'll tell you, there's more personality among that bunch of touring caddies than among the players.

I got my start in golf as a caddie at the Jackson Country Club

48

in Michigan. My folks' farm backed up against the course and I learned to love the game as a caddie, and for that reason I'll always feel a strong empathy for the tour caddies. The young players on tour are coming off the college campuses instead of out of the caddie yards, and I feel sorry for them for what they've missed. Even some of the new young tour caddies are college graduates. That baffles me. Did they major in caddying? Most of the tour caddies got their education on the road.

They all love to travel and love golf, the excitement of the tour, and being outdoors in fresh air. Their reputation, mixed in the past, is getting better. There have been problems in the past because, for example, some caddie would run out of a motel without paying. Now some of the older caddies have taken charge of booking motel rooms for everybody and making sure everybody pays.

There are probably three dozen caddies who travel the tour full-time. They can work almost all the tournaments now with the exception of a handful of summer events that still use local caddies, usually schoolboys on vacation: the clubs feel they owe the work to the local caddies. The tour caddies, on the other hand, contend that when that happens they're being deprived of their livelihood, and I think they're right. Besides, some of these local caddies are a real joke. At Westchester Country Club where the Westchester Classic is played, the caddies are too frequently a bunch of old winos who move so slowly you're afraid you're going to kill one of them when they're shagging balls on the range. If you turned them loose on the first green, they couldn't find the clubhouse. Lee Trevino threatened to skip the tournament unless he could bring his own caddie, and Westchester finally relented and let the tour caddies work.

A tour caddie customarily gets 5 percent of his player's winnings each week plus so much per day or week. I pay my regular caddie 5 percent of what I win plus $150 a week. At the end of the year he'll wind up making better than 10 percent of what I win. And I'm always throwing in a little something extra. When I won a new car in the Buick Open, I gave my year-old car to my caddie at the time, Junior. I helped him with his hospital bills when he had serious throat surgery. He didn't have any health insurance. I loaned him money when he was short, which was most of the time. No matter how well I played, Junior never seemed to have any money. Like a lot of the caddies, he loved to gamble—sometimes I think he lived to gamble.

I've had several good tour caddies, and a good one is well worth the extra several thousand dollars a year I pay. A good tour caddie is worth at least a shot a round to me. Try that on the money list and see what happens—he can pay for himself several times over. He can be the difference between winning and losing.

What does he do for me to be so valuable? First, he's dependable. I don't have to worry about his being late or showing up hung over. Also, he knows the rules and isn't going to get me a stupid two-shot penalty for raking a sand trap before I get in it, for instance, something I've seen local caddies do more than once. He'll always keep my clubs and ball clean. I can trust him. He drives my car and takes care of my kids.

My caddie's week starts when he gets his yardages on Monday and Tuesday. He paces off the course and computes the yardages from the landing areas for tee shots. He picks a spot—a bush or a sprinkler head or whatever—and knows exactly how far that spot is from the center of the green. Then the morning of each round during the tournament, he'll walk the course again to note where the pin position is on each green. Now if I hit into the left rough he can go to his yardage checkpoint, walk off the distance I am from there, evaluate the pin position—and tell me I'm 174 yards from the hole. Not 170 or 180, but 174. That may not sound like a big deal, but I can guarantee you it's crucial when you're trying to select a club, because ten yards can mean you go up or down a club. If I hit a 7-iron to the green when I need a 6-iron, I may well land in water or sand. At one tournament I asked a local caddie how far I was from the pin and he said I was 127 yards. He sounded sure of himself, so I took his word for it. Well, I flew the ball over the green into a jungle and took two more shots getting it on. Later I paced off the distance myself and it came to 106 yards! I reckoned that his mistake in arithmetic cost me $3,000!

Golf has become so scientific that even the top players need all the distance-judging help they can get. Ben Hogan has said that if he could have caddied for Sam Snead, Sam might *never* have lost. I don't think Sam's depth perception has ever been good, even when he was in his prime (the earlier part of his prime, that is), and he's been known to take a 3-iron when he needed a 6-iron and then line the ball off a scoreboard behind the green. Lately Sam has had his caddie get the yardages.

It isn't only yardage, either, but the type of yardage that's important. A top caddie will tell me it's 172 yards but also will caution me quietly that it's uphill and will play more like 182, or he'll remind me that a dip in front of the green makes the distance deceiving, or that the ball is liable to fly out of a fluffy lie and go farther than usual. We'll discuss a shot in detail after he gives me the yardage.

"Is a 5-iron too much?" I might ask.

"You can get there with a 6."

"I want to leave the ball a little short of the hole to avoid a downhill putt."

"The 5 might put you above the hole."

And I probably will go with the 6. I don't want him telling me what club to hit, however. He gives me the yardage and then if I'm undecided on a club I'll ask particular questions and he'll answer them. He doesn't volunteer that kind of information. I tell him not to. I want to form my own impressions first. I'm the one who has to hit the shot.

The average weekend golfer who has trouble breaking 90 underestimates the need to get good yardages. First, he should take the time on the practice range to find out how far he hits each club in his bag, using good balls rather than range balls unless he intends to use range balls in his next game. He plays the same course over and over and it's almost no trouble at all to mark up a scoreboard with landmarks that tell him how far he is from the middle of the green. If you aren't sure you have the right club, it's impossible to hit a shot confidently and get good results. If you're an average golfer, I'm sure a tour caddie could cut six shots off your score just by improving your club selection.

A professional caddie knows me as well as my wife does, better where golf is concerned, and he's something of an amateur psychologist. Club selection can be the smaller part of his contribution compared with how he can assist me mentally. Since I'm an impulsive, fast-moving person, I have a bad tendency to rush things under tournament pressure. Golf is not a game you can rush. For every stroke you try to force out of her, she is going to extract two strokes in return. A tour caddie has his subtle gimmicks to slow me down when I start playing too fast. He'll take extra time getting off the tee or pacing off a yardage. Occasionally he'll even put the bag down for a couple of minutes, and there isn't much I can do without a club.

If I hit a couple of bad shots and get upset with myself, as I invariably will, he'll say something to bring me to my senses like, "Just give me a smooth swing this time. Give me that smooth swing you made on the second tee. That's the one we want every time." He's replaced a negative thought with a positive one, and at this level that's what the game is all about. It's 90 percent mental. A good caddie never shows disappointment. I have a bad habit of jerking the club away from the ball under pressure; this ruins the entire tempo of your swing. Tommy Bolt has a key thought that works for me. He says he knows he's not taking the club away too fast if he can see it go back the first three feet out of the corner of his eye. I might ask my caddie to implant that thought in my mind as I prepare for the shot. He'll know when to say something and when to keep his mouth closed. Lately a friend of mine, Don "Chipmunk" Silvanic, a club pro from Arizona, has been caddying for me. He's an old friend who can keep me loose by telling a joke at the right time. We even kid about "Chester Choke" grabbing me under pressure.

For several years I had my caddie crouch behind the ball when I was putting. Then other players started having their caddies do it. The main purpose was to check my putter alignment. He could tell me whether or not I had the blade lined up. That was a definite plus, because it was one big thing I didn't have to worry about when making my stroke. A secondary gain was that he blocked out crowd movement from my field of vision. Then the rules were changed to keep caddies off the greens because of what I was doing.

Good caddies are more important than jockeys on horses. Also they can adjust from one player to another. Most of the others can't. They either don't give you anything but the yardages or else they want to play the game for you. I'd say there are a half dozen real good caddies on the tour. The rest are just bag-toters. The good ones aren't with the best players in most cases. I don't think Jack Nicklaus asks much of his caddie. They get along well personally and that caddie makes more than a lot of guys on the list of top 60 money winners.

Golfball is a good caddie and so are Frog and Del. You don't deal in last names with the caddies, just first names, and they have some beauties. There's also Turk and Rabbit and Big Fat Mitch and Ol' Roy, and they're every bit as colorful as their names. Rabbit, Gary Player's caddie, is from Harlem and dresses flashier than anybody else on the tour. He's always wanting you to feel a dazzling new pair of expensive slacks he has on. George Plimpton wrote a book about the tour and featured Rabbit, who now fashions himself as something of a star.

Another zany character among the caddies is Poolroom Tom, Chi Chi Rodriguez' caddie and self-appointed "road manager." Tom is a billiards shark from New Jersey who claims to have taken Minnesota Fats after he hustled him by setting up a match where nobody could talk. It turns out Minnesota Fats goes crazy if he can't talk. Poolroom Tom is talking about crusading to become the first white caddie in the Masters Tournament. The Masters always furnishes its own caddies, all black, and Rodriguez has always felt that the big stars get the good caddies there and he is deprived. Poolroom Tom is even more excitable than Chi Chi; at Atlanta one year after a round he picked a fight with Larry Ziegler, who had played with Chi Chi. Ziegler is about twice his size and strong enough to be a heavyweight boxer, and Poolroom Tom is lucky he didn't get killed. I heard he hit Larry with a putter and ran—not a bad thing to do if you've been foolish enough to hit Larry with a putter.

The all-time character, though, was a caddie who worked off and on for Orville Moody. He was in the Army with Orville. He had boxes full of cards with yardages that he kept tucked away in safe deposit boxes in a bank. He would practice his pacing stride on a football field by the hour. When he went into a shoe store he wouldn't buy a new pair of shoes until he was convinced he could pace off an exact yard in them. One time during the Crosby Tournament he had a dream that he had a bad yardage on a hole, so he got up at 2 A.M., and drove to the course, and repaced the hole with a flashlight. Another time he informed Orville, dead serious, that a course was 133 feet longer than it had been the year before. Then there was the time at Indian Wells in Palm Springs that he walked through a water hazard up to his neck to get his yardage on a straight line from tee to green. He was unbelievable. You had to say he was dedicated to his job.

Caddying isn't an easy job for anybody. Those big modern golf bags weigh upwards of a hundred pounds when you pack them as full as we do. A caddie is up at daybreak to get his pin positions and he usually has to shag balls for an hour before the round and an hour afterward, at least. I've stayed on the practice range for five hours after a round trying to work out a

54

problem, beating balls. George Archer is another great practicer, and to beat the monotony his caddie has taken to wearing a first baseman's glove and fielding George's shots on the range. He makes some plays Brooks Robinson would be proud of, even catching a drive behind his back. He once caught 50 drives in a row—and George doesn't drive it that straight.

The caddies drive our cars while we fly. To hold down expenses they often will sleep five and six to a room in a budget motel, eat at out-of-the-way cafeterias, and hitchhike to the course. They work hard, most of them, and that's why it bugs hell out of me when some pious critic says they shouldn't be allowed to travel the tour. Gene Sarazen says he's afraid a tour caddie might cheat to help his employer. Sarazen is always looking for an angle to keep his name in the papers, which is fine because the game can always use his flavor, but he makes no sense here. No caddie can get away with anything his player doesn't want him to get away with, and the player's honesty is the foundation of the sport. I don't know a tour caddie who would resort to cheating anyway. Their jobs are on the line and they're smarter than that. Some of the younger players argue that only the top players can afford tour caddies and that isn't fair to the ones who can't. That's like saying only the top players can afford to travel first class and therefore have an advantage. Sure they do, but it's the type of advantage that goes with having worked your way to the top. Nobody starts out at the top.

I think that problem will work itself out as more and more good, bright young caddies join the tour and pick up with the younger players. The Tournament Players Division is talking about accrediting the caddies just as it qualifies and accredits the players. That's a good idea. But I hope the TPD doesn't try to bleach all the color out of them and turn them into a bunch of dull conformists like service station attendants—and like most of the players. The tour would be much less fun for me to play. I don't know where I'd go for a quick laugh and a dose of reality.

EARLY LIFE

As you get older you stop and ask yourself why you are who you are. What shaped your personality? In my case, I have to wonder what has made me so strongly individualistic, so outspoken and controversial. That's my public image. There are other sides to me that I wonder about too.

Whenever I reflect on my golf career and my life in general I think back to my father. He had more to do with my amounting to something than anybody else, and from him I got my self-reliance. I don't think I ever could come close to being as good a man as my father was, because I don't have the compassion for people that he always had. He and I were totally unlike in some ways. But the good qualities I have I owe to him.

My father died in 1963 at the early age of 58. I was in Salt Lake City for a golf tournament. He had been sick for several years and didn't want the family to wait around for him to die.

He wanted me to be out playing the tour—he got great satisfaction out of my golf career, which he had made possible but never took credit for.

His death had a lasting effect on me. It gave me a whole different approach to life. Now I look on each new day as a bonus. I figure I might die tomorrow so I'd better try to use today to make up for what went wrong yesterday and not worry about the future. I handle my own problems—for right or wrong—and if I make enemies, I don't care. I either like you or I don't like you, and if you ask me which category you fall into I will be glad to tell you.

If you ask me a question, I am going to answer it. If the answer offends you, that's not my problem. I say what I feel. If you bug me, I'll insult you and then forget about it. Many people resent my attitude. Many are jealous; they'd like to say what they think but are afraid to.

I believe that if I live my life like this, I am ready to die tomorrow. I'm not religious in the sense of practicing an organized faith, but I'm religious in my own fashion. I believe that when I die, I'm going to be with my father again, and that's something to look forward to. I didn't realize how much I thought of my father—how much I loved him—until he was dead.

My father literally worked himself to death. I learned to work hard from my father, with a difference. I decided after watching him work two and three jobs a day doing things he couldn't enjoy that I was going to work at what I wanted to work at. Our family never had much money and Dad worked full shifts for the post office in the daytime and in a building-supplies factory at night, and he also took on free-lance accounting jobs. We never lacked good shelter and good food and good clothes, plus extras like a big Christmas. Dad deprived himself—he would buy a pair of shoes only once every three or four years—but he made sure he didn't deprive the rest of us. There were six of us kids and he had to struggle 16 and 18 hours a day to provide for us. He never complained.

He used to take us with him in the summer on his mail route, Route 8. He would come home and pick us up after he cased his route. You case your route down at the post office, sorting the mail into bundles in the order you are going to deliver it. Dad would drive his own car on the route, which was a pretty wild route out in the country, mostly farm homes, including our own. We lived about four miles outside the city limits of Jackson, Michigan. Most of the small farmers have gone out of business now.

We kids would sit in the back and Dad would use the entire front seat. It was a great show watching him work. He'd sit toward the middle of the seat. The right window was down so he could reach out to stuff the mail in the boxes by the road. He didn't have an automatic transmission and he would shift and steer with his left hand and work the gas pedal, brake and clutch with his left foot. He could drop off the mail almost without bringing the car to a stop.

On top of that he would read the morning paper while driving his route, balancing it in his lap! He'd have the entire paper read by the time we got home. He worried me driving along those narrow dirt roads at 45 and 50 miles an hour reading the paper, but he knew those roads as well as a blind man knows the hallway in his boarding house. There wasn't any traffic and he never hit anything, except an occasional duck or chicken that wandered out into the road.

Dad also worked our 60-acre farm. When I was little, we had sixteen head of dairy cattle and all the equipment to milk them, but the dairy end of it got to be too much for him with his other jobs. Dad raised pigs and we had three riding horses that we grew up on. It was a well-rounded farm. The kids all pitched in to keep the vegetable patches clean. We would hoe so many rows of corn or whatever each day. I was too young to bale hay and tried to dodge any other work I could.

58

There was a lot of fun in growing up on a farm. During hay-cutting season we would pull the loaded hay wagon under the door in the top of the barn and then bail out of the door into the hay. It was probably only 20 feet down but it seemed like 80 to a little kid. When Dad was plowing we'd run along barefooted behind him and the plow would turn the dirt over on our feet. That was the greatest sensation in the world. I feel sorry for kids who grow up in a big city and never know the simple pleasures of living on a farm. Kids can really learn how to live in the country.

Dad did everything himself. He even built our house, a big colonial brick home that is going to be standing long after I'm dead. It has three stories and a basement and I wish my expensive home was built as solidly. Dad and some friends put thick tile on the outside and brick on the tile and plaster on the brick. It's no hovel inside, either. The ceilings are beamed —Dad cut the wood himself—and the flooring is walnut and oak and black cherry. The Jackson Country Club bordered on our property and Dad got most of the wood there. The club wanted to build an entranceway across the corner of our property and Dad gave his permission in exchange for the trees that came down. What wood he didn't use building the house, he sawed up and burned in the furnace in the winter to save money on coal.

We later learned, from the autopsy after his death, that Dad had done much of this hard work with a back broken in two places. He was in pain for years and still put in his long days and never missed a day of work until he got so sick he couldn't continue. He was unbelievably strong. He wasn't that big —5'10" and 180 pounds—but I have seen him heft a log 2 feet around and 30 feet long onto each shoulder and walk across the farm with them.

Dad had no hobbies as such. He played a little cards and pool and liked to raise flowers, especially red roses, and hunt pheasant in the fall, but his time was pretty well taken up with working and he didn't get much sleep as it was. His enjoyment came from helping his family. No matter how busy or tired he was, he always went out of his way to be sure we kids were able to participate in sports. He would finish with his mail route and pick us up to take us to basketball practice or wherever we wanted to go in town.

My older brother, George, a lawyer now, played football in high school, and I don't think Dad ever missed a practice he possibly could attend, let alone a game. Even if he could be there only fifteen minutes, he'd go out and watch George practice when he should have been home sleeping before he went to his factory job at ten o'clock at night.

He was often more of a father to other kids on our teams than their own fathers were. He was always the first father to volunteer to drive a carload of kids to a game, and after the game he would treat everybody to hot dogs and soft drinks. My father would spend the last few dollars in his pocket on those refreshments. He did that all through my grade school, junior high, and high school days. Those kids didn't realize what a friend they had in my Dad. It scalded my ass when only a couple of them showed up at his funeral.

Dad always encouraged my younger brother Mike and me with our golf. He never played much himself, three or four holes with us in the evening now and then. When we were caddying at the country club he would pick us up when we were through and take us to the public course in Al Sharp Park several miles away, and we'd play until it got dark. He'd wait for us, and sometimes we'd stay and putt on the practice green by the lights of his car.

When we started playing in junior tournaments and then high school tournaments, we weren't old enough to drive, but Dad always made sure to take us and pick us up, and to follow us for a few holes. I was nine years old when I played in my first tournament, and Dad caddied for me. I'll never forget that match. I was barely four feet tall and the other kid was

60

six-feet-six. We went twenty holes. The last hole was about a 165-yard carry over water and I couldn't fly the ball that far so I had to go the long way around the water and I lost. Dad pepped me up and told me I was going to win tournaments when I got bigger.

Dad was right, whether he knew it or not, and I just wish he could have seen more of them. By the time I was playing well on the tour he was too sick to come out and watch me. We used to play the Buick Open in Michigan and he would come up for a day or two, but he was awfully sick. He was proud of Mike and me being on the tour, though. I don't know how we ever could thank him for making it possible. He gave us every chance to do what we wanted to do.

He set a terrific example for us. I just wish I were more like him. He was generous to complete strangers, down to his last dollar. One Sunday afternoon in the fall, we all had been raking leaves and were eating chicken and dumplings outside. A Mexican farm laborer came up the driveway and asked for something to eat. Dad didn't know him from a load of coal. But Dad sat him down at the table and fed him all he could eat. Then Dad asked him if he had any money. The man said he didn't. Dad gave him his last twenty dollar bill. Then Dad asked him if he had work. The man said no again. Dad drove him downtown and got him a free place to sleep. The next day Dad helped find him a job at a local hardware store. The man stayed around Jackson for years and was a good citizen. Dad did things like that many a time.

I never heard him say anything bad about anybody. If he didn't like someone, he didn't say anything at all. I saw him in only one argument all my life, over a business deal with my uncle, and he forgot it as soon as it ended. He couldn't carry a grudge.

He disciplined us kids when we needed a swat in the ass. My mother tells me he used to say he hated to punish me because I stayed mad. He did me a lot of good by disciplining me. I knew when he told me something he meant it, and I rarely went against him. If he told me to be home from a high school dance by midnight, it didn't even occur to me to stay out later than that. If you were roughhousing and bothering him —we'd let the hide go with the hair—he'd nail you with a good wallop in the ass, but five minutes after he had punished you he was your pal again. He'd ask you if you wanted to ride down to the combination filling station and grocery store with him and he'd give you two cents to buy a candy bar (fifteen cents today). He was a helluva man, as good a father as you could have. When Joe Dey was commissioner and tried to give me a "fatherly talk" I told him I had a father who was the best.

We kids didn't backtalk him and we didn't backtalk our mother, because if we did, we were going to wish we had kept our mouths shut. I haven't said enough about Mom. She looks like Santa Claus' wife today but she has plenty of flint in her. She lived her life in that big brick house, going shopping only once or twice a month, and she could cook better than the head chef at the Waldorf, good solid meals. We always had homemade bread and fresh vegetables and good meat. She would bake six or seven loaves of bread a day. She says the reason I didn't weigh 100 pounds until I was over sixteen was that I didn't eat enough of her bread and taters. She's probably right. Mike brings Mom to Doral in Florida for the tournament every year, and she's critical of the food there, but I'll have to admit she can do better.

Mom will remind Mike and me of the time she and Dad were away and we took it on ourselves to paint the fence and wagon and garage the worst shade of brown you can imagine. Or the time we chased a sow around a corner of the house and he ran between the legs of a neighbor lady who probably hasn't recovered to this day. She says our wings just never quite sprouted. But she says it with a glitter in her eye. Mom's younger than a lot of 25-year-olds I know.

I never got an allowance when I was a kid. Dad didn't

believe in allowances. The kids all worked—my sisters sold our vegetables at roadside stands—and all the money went into a pool. We paid for our school clothes and books out of that pool. If Dad and Mom needed some of that money to cover household expenses, they were welcome to it. They always asked first.

We damn sure weren't spoiled and I'm glad of it. I'm not about to spoil my three kids either. I'm not going to break their spirit, but I'm not going to take any crap from them. I play golf with them and insist on good etiquette. One of them threw a tantrum and broke an iron one day and I gave him fourteen kinds of hell. There I was, the last of the angry old men, disciplining my young son for a temper display! But I'm determined that those kids grow up right.

Once they're of legal age they can go on their way. If I have supported and raised them to that point, they can walk out the front door and say good-bye because they are their own people if I have done my job. They should be able to handle their own problems and earn their own keep. They'll have to make it on their own, and the sooner they start, the better off they'll be.

I don't expect them to take care of me when I'm older. That would be asking too much of them when they have their own lives to live. My brother Mike did much more for our folks than I did after we were of age. When the rest of us took off, he stayed behind and took care of Mom and Dad and the farm. He drove a beer truck and did the plowing and cut the wood and handled the livestock. He just wouldn't leave. He loves farmwork. He married a farmer's daughter and is saving his money on the tour to buy a farm and settle down. He's really a solid person, a lot solider than I am.

Growing up, Mike was my only friend. We put on the boxing gloves when we were little kids and landed a lot of powder-puff punches, but it was always in fun and we were always very close. He could whip everybody in the tough end of town we had to walk through to get to and from school, and I learned early that I wanted him on my side.

The other kids picked on me because I stuttered badly in school until the eighth grade, from nervousness. At home I was fine, but in school I couldn't put three words together without getting my tongue tangled. The other kids rode me unmercifully about my stuttering. It's beyond me how kids can be that nasty to somebody who has a handicap, and today if I hear somebody chiding a handicapped person, I turn livid.

The stuttering made me a terrible loner, which caused the bullies to pick on me all the more. I hate to think of the beatings I'd have taken if Mike and his strong left hook hadn't been alongside me. He could dust anybody.

Mike wasn't that much bigger than I was then, but today he's 180 pounds and hard as a rock pile, and meaner than he ever was. Everybody thinks I'm the mean one of the family, but that's just because they don't know Mike that well. He won't let them get close enough to know him. I used to fight him, but I would never take him on now. Mike is a great guy, but he can come with some awfully short answers. He cannot stand bullshit. He is a private kind of man, quiet and shy, and he does not look kindly on people who intrude on his privacy with foolish talk. I wouldn't say Mike doesn't like people, but he definitely doesn't like people who invite themselves to his table in a bar. You see people doing that everywhere on the tour, trying to make small talk with the golfers. Mike has always said that if he wants you at his table, he'll ask you over.

If these phonies knew Mike, they'd stay away from him, because he can be some kind of mean. He would always give a bad actor a warning—tell him to take a walk—and then lay one on him. But after he put in 42 months in the Air Force and drove the beer truck in Jackson, I noticed a difference in his attitude. After that, he wouldn't even tell the guy he was bugging him, he'd just lay him out. He got terribly strong working on the farm and hefting those big kegs of beer, and it seemed that the stronger he got, the meaner he got. He had a couple of scrapes in Jackson that they're still talking about.

One night he was sitting in a bar drinking beer and talking to someone and a guy sat down on the other side of him and ordered a beer. The bartender set up the beer and the guy promptly spilled it. It got on Mike's arm. Mike brushed the beer off his arm and turned his head to look at the guy, without saying anything. The bartender wiped up the mess with the bar rag and set up another beer for the guy. Damned if he didn't spill the second beer, too, and it ran down into Mike's lap. Mike said "Pardon me" to the man he was talking to, turned around and slugged the guy off his stool onto the floor. The guy had no more than hit the floor when Mike put a foot on his throat, leaned down, and said, "Mister, that's for not excusing yourself for spilling the first beer. When you get up, you've got another one coming for not excusing yourself for spilling the second one."

Don't get the wrong idea about Mike. He's no hood and he's no brawler. He'd never lay a hand on anyone unless he was provoked. But if he's provoked, you'd better give him plenty of room.

He's the ideal husband. He's married to a pretty blonde and I've never heard him raise his voice to her. They have three pleasant kids. Mike loves to work around the house and can fix anything that goes wrong. He manages his money well and is saving and planning for that farm he wants to own.

He hasn't made a pile of money on the tour, but he stays in the top 60 and wins tournaments, and his best years are still ahead of him. We started playing golf at the same time as kids, but he hasn't played one-tenth as much as I have over the years. He was more interested in baseball while he was growing up and he didn't play that much in the Air Force or while he was working at home. I came on the tour in 1959 but Mike didn't come out until 1968.

I often wonder how good he might be if he had taken the

game seriously sooner. He probably would be better than I am. He's much stronger, and his swing is more solid. He takes the club away from the ball farther inside the target line than I do, doesn't take it back as far, and makes a great move back to the ball with his legs. He isn't as technically minded as I am.

Mike is a ferocious competitor. In 1971 he was 98th on the money list in late July and felt he had to make the top 60 or give up the tour. He made money in eleven of the last twelve tournaments, breaking par 24 times in 34 rounds, and moved up all the way to 55th place.

Mike is more conservative than I am. The first two rounds he plays to make the cut and the last two rounds he plays to make money. I tend to let it all hang out from the start, and if things don't go well I might just drop out and go on down the road. With his conservatism and my boldness, we make a compatible best-ball team. We tied for fifth one year in a national team championship on the tour and we did well in the CBS Classic.

I feel bad that Mike has been in my shadow on the tour. He's had to take a lot of stuff from people over the years, but he's never complained. We don't compete against each other out here. I give him lessons. When he wins a tournament, I'm happier than he is. We've been each other's biggest booster since we started in sports.

We first were exposed to golf together when I was five. The sixth hole of the Jackson Country Club course, a tricky par-3, played right up against the back of our farm. A large maple tree, with branches that drooped almost to the ground, stood behind the green on our property, and we would sit under the tree on summer days and watch the club members play up. If they missed the green to the left, their balls would go into the woods. When they lost a ball, we would wait until they had moved on to the next hole and then we'd go find it. We collected many a ball, and Dad would take them down to the post office and sell them.

We did that for a couple of summers. Mike was drifting more and more into baseball but my older brother George was a caddie at the club, and when I was seven I went over there and asked to caddie. I was told I was too small. I'm not sure how big I was then, but I was smaller than a golf bag. So for two summers I was the official shag boy at the club instead, chasing down the lesson balls all day. When the pro played he let me pull his bag on a cart.

Finally, when I was nine, I was allowed to caddie. The best part about caddying was getting to play golf every Monday, caddie's day. The pro cut down a wood, an iron, and a putter for me, old wooden-shafted clubs, and that was as good a starter set as I could have asked for. We'd get up and tee off at 6 A.M. on Monday and play until we got run off, usually around noon. The other days George and I would caddie and then hit shots back and forth in the farmyard. I would race through my chores to play golf. Mom says the mower never hit the ground when I cut the yard.

I took to the game pretty naturally. I could get the ball airborne right away. I couldn't hit it far enough to lose it, I was so small, but I suspect my form was not bad. I could break 100 that first year. I learned the basics of swinging a golf club mostly by imitation. The pro showed me how to put my hands on the club, and I think that's about all any kid needs. You can develop your own swing, and usually it's the swing that best suits your build and temperament. I caddied for some of the good players around Jackson and picked up a lot just observing them and then trying to mimic them. It's amazing how a kid can see something as complicated as a golf swing and go out himself and visualize it and almost duplicate it with a little practice. I'm glad I learned to swing by myself. I'm confident in my basic swing. We've been through a lot together. I've never been tempted to start copying other pros' swings. You would be astonished how many promising players screw up their games that way.

I started playing in tournaments when I was nine and had a good peewee record. I suppose kids can start competing seriously too soon, but it sure helped me more than it hurt me to start early. You learn to compete by competing and experiencing the disappointment of losing and the joy of winning, and you can be ready for that at nine. I was never pushed into competing, though, and I would never push my kids into playing a sport they didn't care to play. They'd be psychologically behind from the start.

I played football and basketball in high school in addition to golf. I wasn't worth a damn at football—I never rose above the third team—but I enjoyed the physical contact. I always had a four-alarm temper, which Dad gave me plenty of hell about, and in football I could get mad and take it out on somebody. If I had grown to be six-feet-four and 250 pounds, I might have been the scourge of the National Football League. As it was, at St. Mary's High School I was a 90-pound linebacker whose bark was worse than his bite.

I wasn't afraid to tackle anybody and I would sneak up into the line to be sure I got some action. I was one of those idiots who enjoyed the midweek intrasquad scrimmages as much as I did the games, just so long as I could whack people. But once I had busted a ball carrier, I still had the problem of bringing him down. I can remember being dragged fifteen yards by a big fullback in one game—I must have looked like a toy terrier that had got hold of somebody's pants leg. My main job in the games was to hold the ball for our team's kickoffs.

I was much better at basketball than football. I did about as much hitting too. Nobody ever told me basketball was a noncontact sport. I was never thrown out of a football game, but I was thrown out of basketball games. I was a little pecker, and I figured I had to play aggressively or I would be run off the court. Usually I didn't get nasty until somebody got nasty with me, but I evened most scores physically.

I learned to use my sharp little elbows quite adroitly and

found that, as a little man, I could get away with more under the basket than a big man because the referee couldn't see me. I was an all-star grabber. I grabbed my opponent's shirt or pants or whatever was handy to hold him in check. Once in a while I got caught, but I tried to save my major retaliations for the last few seconds of the game when it wouldn't make any difference if I was ejected. In those small gyms we played in, there would be a wall right behind the baseline. Sometimes it was padded and sometimes it wasn't. If I owed a man a dirty trick, I was known to run him into the wall as he was leaping to shoot a layup. That could smart.

For a $1.50 bet one game I slugged the husky center on the opposing team. We were down on the floor wrestling for the ball, and I didn't think the referee could see us, so I put my arm around the big center's head, locked him in, and gave him a shot in the face. I looked up—and looking down at me was the referee. I told him I couldn't punch hard enough to hurt anybody, which was true, but he didn't buy it.

I never seemed to make it through a basketball game. I fouled out of three out of every five games. I wasn't a really good shooter, but I made an all-state team, for my hustle as much as anything.

Basketball was a great help to my golf. It improved my coordination and strengthened my legs. I've always been a legs player in golf.

My competitive spirit certainly was better suited to football and basketball. When I get mad on the golf course, which is frequently, I feel mean and want to fight. But I can't. Not that I'd ever whip anybody. I've had probably 400 fights in my life and haven't won one yet, and if I ever find that cat I can whup, I'm going to sign him up and cart him around the country with me: I'd be able to release the pressures that build up inside me. In golf you have to choke back that mean streak.

TRAVEL-SEX-MARRIAGE

The travel on the tour keeps an added strain on you. The glamour wears off fast. It's a different city every week for golfers—you never have a home game—and you rarely see any sights except the golf course.

I leave town the minute a tournament's over and my golf bag is packed. I never stay Sunday night. The week is over as soon as your last putt drops, and you start thinking about going down the road. It drags you down after a few weeks. You're changing climate so much and sleeping in rooms where the air conditioning is too high or too low, and you seem to be vulnerable to every virus in the air. Personal problems are always exaggerated under conditions this unstable.

When I first turned pro, I wasn't sure I'd have enough money to get from one place to the next. I remember in 1959 I drove down to College Station, Texas, where Henry Ransom was coaching Texas A & M. Henry was helping me with my game.

It was three days before Christmas. I had my first wife and my little daughter with me, and I didn't have a penny for presents for them. I entered a pro-am down there at the last minute and teed off late in the afternoon. I had a good round going, but it was getting dark fast and I didn't know if I'd be able to finish. A couple of foursomes let my group play through because I had a chance to win low pro. I came in with a 65, I think it was, and won $200 and that was our Christmas money. Then my little girl burned herself and we had to take her to the hospital.

One time in Phoenix we had a cheap motel room with a gas oven. I was going to light the gas, but I didn't know what I was doing. I turned up the gas and stuck a match in there. The explosion ripped the door off the stove and I was blown darn near through the wall.

Another time, my wife was driving across California to meet me, and she had a miscarriage. We were lucky. Her doctor was in Los Angeles at the time and he treated her. The next day she drove six hours to the tournament.

Late one night we were driving from San Diego to Pebble Beach on Route 1 and we got lost and wound up on the wrong road. We were on a winding, narrow stretch that hangs right out over the ocean. It's so dangerous the cops don't even patrol it after dark. The wind was blowing and it started raining and I thought it was all over. We made it on one windshield wiper and a prayer.

The pros have had a lot of close calls driving from tournament to tournament. George Knudson once was traveling with his wife and kids when his car burst into flames on the highway. Fortunately, nobody was seriously hurt.

The pros have always liked big, fast cars in order to make long drives as comfortable as possible. It can take three days to get from California to Florida, and that's exhausting. I don't know what the tour record is for speeding tickets, but it could be the seven that the late Bo Wininger got driving from Texas to New Orleans in the old days.

Nowadays anybody who makes the top 60 can afford to fly, maybe first class. Or you can afford to fly if you're a young kid with a rich sponsor. TF—Tour Fatigue—doesn't catch up to you quite as fast when you travel by plane. I fly about a hundred thousand miles a year, and I've never had a bad flight.

My first wife traveled with me quite a bit when the kids weren't in school, but the golf tour doesn't do much to help your sex life, or your marriage or family life in general. I'm sure it contributed heavily to the breakup of my first marriage.

I suppose tour wives are no worse than any other wives, but too many of them second-guess their husbands' golf and spend the day gossiping with each other around the swimming pool. Naturally there are some good wives, but they're in the minority. You'll never catch me hitting practice balls with a woman sitting on my golf bag. I've seen a golfer's wife give him hell at the top of her voice for 3-putting when he came off the last green. As if he wanted to 3-putt!

A couple of pros' wives have put them smack into bankruptcy in recent years. Some of these wives travel from one swish country club to another and decide they need to lead that kind of life. The pros have a good year and their wives immediately want to move out of a $40,000 house into a $175,000 house. They want new wardrobes and new cars and maids and first-class airfare to all the tournaments. Those wives don't realize that one good year doesn't make you rich. Next year you might not make the top 60. You can win a major championship and a $40,000 check and where do you think that money is going to take you? Uncle Sam gets his share, and a business manager gets his, and you subtract your expenses, and what's left is going to take you only down the road to the next tournament.

Fans forget that golfers have to maintain a home and still pay their expenses while traveling to expensive resort areas. Your bills at home can be a thousand dollars a month, and if your wife's with you on tour you're looking at another thousand a month. Have a bad year and your standard of living can shoot down like a broken elevator. Traveling with your wife can take the chanciness out of your sex life, but you're going to spend a lot of money on her.

Dan Jenkins wrote a golf novel that was mostly about sex, and one player was making it with another player's wife. That's one thing I haven't seen out here. Some guys fool around—the same as some insurance salesmen or firemen or college professors—but not with each other's wives, not that I've noticed. And I'm sure you'd hear about it. The tour is too much a little world of its own, even moving around the country. Maybe golfers and their wives are too well aware of the difficulties that would follow. Or maybe they're intimidated by the gossip syndrome. If a married golfer is seen with a strange woman, everybody on the tour is liable to know about it inside of twelve hours. One married player for several years had a thing going with a southern schoolteacher, and he would fly her out to a dozen tournaments a year—his caddie estimates the guy spent $15,000 on this woman one season. The player went to incredible lengths to avoid being caught by the other wives. He would find out where all the players were staying and then book a room clear across town, an hour and a half from the golf course instead of ten minutes. He would eat at restaurants up on mountain tops at midnight. She would go to the tournament and follow him occasionally, but they'd never give any sign they even knew each other. He was sure he was keeping the biggest secret in the world —and every wife on the tour knew exactly what he was doing.

73

My favorite story about sex and the golf tour features a top player who was asleep with his wife in a Fort Worth motel room at 3 A.M. when they heard loud knocking at the door. They woke up and he opened the door, and there was a sensational looking blonde, built like a brick henhouse, completely nude. He got rid of her, but not before his wife saw her. He told his wife the blonde was walking in her sleep. The funny part is that the blonde really was walking in her sleep—but can you imagine the trouble the guy had convincing his wife of that?

I imagine the tour attracts more beautiful women than any other sport. At least they're closer to the players. A football player isn't going to notice a good-looking girl sitting in Section E during a game, but a golfer has plenty of time to scan the galleries while he's playing. I don't know of an easier way to lose your concentration. After you play you'll have a sandwich and a few drinks in the clubhouse, and good-looking girls will be everywhere you turn. Over all, golf appeals to a higher-class woman than other sports, with the possible exception of tennis, another country club game.

I've noticed several distinct types of women available to golfers. Many of them don't even play golf, but the tournament may be the only game in town that week, the social event of the season in many cities, and they want to be part of the action.

One type is the country club wife. She's a little older, in her late thirties or forties, and she's looking for a change of pace. You can meet her at a sponsor's party. Her husband is a rich doctor or lawyer and he's too busy making money and being a big shot in the community to take care of her needs. She likes younger men, and she figures a quiet fling with a golfer is safe because he'll be gone next week. You can find some classy women in this category. Some of the married tour players who play around—I doubt that the percentage is any greater than among any other group of men, but golfers certainly are as

74

human as the next fellows about sex—believe the country club wife is the best pairing for the week. She's experienced and doesn't expect a lot of juvenile convincing to make love, and she has too much to lose to spread stories about the golfer.

Occasionally golfers have been caught by irate husbands. One top player will never return to a certain tournament because of a promise made to him that he will be shot on the course if he does. I have never quite understood a man reacting with that attitude, because it takes two to tango, and the golfer probably did not make the first move.

Another type of available woman is the single working girl, the secretary or switchboard operator or receptionist. She's younger and wilder and wants to party half the night. She's bolder than the country club wife; she can afford to be. She's liable to slip your caddie a note with a phone number on it as you go through the crowd to get from one green to the next tee. "Hi—I'm in the yellow halter and shorts—if you're not doing anything tonight, call me at 861-2334 and we'll have some fun." I'm not saying this happens very often to me, but it happens. These girls are looking for a dash of spice in their routine and they somehow have come to the conclusion that professional golfers are glamorous figures, traveling all over the world and making a fortune and wearing bright clothes. I wish they were correct.

Women who work on the tournament have a keener interest in golf. They play the game and know more about the players. They volunteer to keep score and work in the press room and drive the courtesy cars that shuttle the players from their motels to the course and back. You have to be grateful to them. Without them, there would be no tournaments. Sometimes a player will be extra grateful and strike up a close relationship with one of these women. The courtesy car drivers in one midwestern city are known for their willingness to perform above and beyond the call of duty. It has happened there that a driver took two hours to return a player to his motel when the round trip was only five miles on an express-way.

Then there are the girls who work at the club, as waitresses and what have you. They hear so many bad lines that by the middle of the week I'm amazed they even want to look at a man. I remember one player, a Masters champion, who always led into a conversation by asking the girl if she'd like to come over after she got off work and do his laundry. I don't think it ever worked.

The girls you don't fool, of course, are the prostitutes who hang around the tournaments and the motels and hotels that get the tournament traffic. In Augusta the hookers come in from Atlanta for the week by the busload. They go around knocking on doors at the motels soliciting business, at prices from $15 up. I don't have anything against hookers phil-osophically. At least they're honest and they're cleaner than a lot of so-called nice girls.

Golfers are around stewardesses frequently, but I think they're the most overrated group of women in the world. Not one in twenty is really attractive. They have those cardboard personalities. Most of them talk alike, in schoolgirl cli-chés—and I'd bet they're about as exciting in bed. I heard of one stewardess who flew into the sack with a guy two drinks after she'd met him, and when she got up to go early the next morning, half asleep, she mumbled a perfunctory "Thanks for flying United." I know there are exceptions, but that's an accurate generalization. Usually they're after an expensive night out on the town. They don't like to fly into a lively city and then be stuck in a hotel room with a couple of other stews, and they'd prefer to go to the swankiest nightclubs, especially if somebody else is paying.

We have one guy on the tour who is always bragging about how many stews he's seduced under challenging conditions. You've probably heard of the Mile High Club, which has a membership of people who have made it in a plane at an altitude at least that high. This guy claims he's seduced stewardesses at a thousand feet in the galley, in his seat, in the restrooms, you name the setting. The towns where stewardesses are based are always a favorite stop for this guy. He can't wait to get to Miami because hundreds of stews live there. They're off work more than they're on duty, and he's in hog heaven. In the good towns you wouldn't have to go for stewardesses; there are plenty of more interesting girls.

Atlanta is a great town for a single guy, full of available young girls who have come to the big metropolis from the country and want to make up for lost time. Southern girls are warmer anyway. Houston is a good city for girls and so is Memphis, but the best is Fort Worth. I've never seen anything like the Colonial Invitation Tournament down there in May. It's a combination happening/fashion show/week-long party. There are hundreds of knockout girls dressing their sexiest, which means wearing as little as possible in most cases, and drinking and trying to have as good a time as they possibly can. Working girls take a week's vacation to enjoy the tournament. It has all the colorful atmosphere of a sports car race. The tour wives try to make it a point to accompany their husbands to Fort Worth just in case.

Some of my single friends on tour say the worst city for girls is Miami, with Jacksonville and New Orleans right behind. With a big navy base, Jacksonville has the most dirty women: you could catch anything there. They wouldn't go to bed with anybody but a nurse in Jacksonville. Miami's worse because it's an old folks home. The average temperature is 85 and so is the average age. I don't know what's wrong with New Orleans. I love the place for its old Dixieland jazz, but the girls are mostly 1.5 on a scale from zero to 10. The only way to do well in New Orleans is to bring your own.

Before he was married, Ray Floyd was always widely admired for flying in his own beautiful dates, clear across the country if necessary. Ray lived in San Francisco in the lively

North Beach area, where he owned a topless girls' musical group and was friends with Carol Doda, the original silicone girl.

From what I gather, nobody on the golf tour today could have kept up with Bobby Riggs in his tennis prime. I know people who have seen Riggs traveling in the steady company of not one girl—or "bird," as he likes to call a female companion—but of three. He could do that and be a champion, but I don't know anybody else who could. Sam Snead once told me that his three keys to success in golf were: (1) don't swim, (2) don't do pushups, and (3) don't have sex after Wednesday.

Golf and sex don't mix that well. I don't think sex is that good for your legs, and in golf you get your strength from your legs. You're on the course for four or five hours, and just walking the last three holes can be an awful drag when you're under pressure. Sex has caused a lot of bogeys down the stretch and ended a lot of golf careers prematurely.

I know other golfers have different views on how sex affects their play. Doug Sanders has said he likes to have sex and a hot tub bath every morning and he's loose and ready to go. Of course if Sanders had scored half as often with women as he claims he has, he'd be dead. I think he's a poor excuse for a sex symbol with his grey hair and his paunch and his garish clothes. Nobody who talks about his sexual achievements as much as Sanders can be that good.

Tommy Bolt says he has shot many a 67 and 68—no, I'm not going to add 69—after pre-round intercourse. He contends it's the best thing in the world for smoothing out your swing tempo. I don't know anybody with smoother tempo than Tommy, unless it's Gene Littler. I've never heard Gene discuss sex, probably because he has more tact than most of the rest of us and is a perfect family man. One year at a PGA Championship a sensationally constructed girl wiggled out to the practice tee. Everybody stopped hitting and gawked at her.

"Who's she with?" one player wondered.

"Littler," cracked George Archer. Everybody broke up.

I've talked to medical people about sex and golf. One doctor told me sex at bedtime can help you sleep soundly. He said he knows a major league baseball pitcher whose routine calls for sex the night before he's due to pitch. The pitcher believes sex keeps his sinker ball low. This doctor concludes that there's no established correlation between sex and athletic performance but that sex is more apt to hurt single athletes than married athletes. His theory is that the single athlete is more likely to run himself down chasing girls and drinking and staying up all night. Once you've caught a girl, he says, the sex itself is not that tiring.

A lot depends on your priorities. To me getting laid is no major accomplishment. While I am getting laid, probably 400 million other people around the world are getting laid too. Big deal. I've never found sex that exciting, not nearly as exciting as golf. To me golf comes first and sex is down the list somewhere. Give me par scores or better the rest of my life and I'll give you all the sex I'm going to get without a second thought. It isn't every day that you can go out and shoot a 67 or 68, but you don't have to be very special to get laid every day. You have to be persistent more than anything else.

Sex has more to do with the booming popularity of the men's tour than you might think. At least half of Arnold Palmer's popularity has always been in his sex appeal. The next time you have a chance, notice how many women of all ages are in his gallery and check their reactions when he does something forcefully masculine or starts counting the house while waiting to putt.

Jack Nicklaus has become much more sexually attractive in the last few years. He slimmed down and let his hair grow and started dressing better, and all of a sudden the girls started warming to him. His wife Barbara saw what was happening and she lost weight and sharpened up herself. She's a super gal, and you can tell she keeps Jack happy.

Sex can be available as a lure to get a top player into a tournament now and again. The player is given to understand that if he plays in the Greater Waterbed Classic, he can have the company of a beautiful girl in a private home for the week. There is a girl who carries the title of social director at a resort that plays host to a tournament, and believe me she can socialize with the best of them. The top players, though, are so wealthy today that they can be above almost any sort of enticement, including sex, and they play the tournaments they enjoy playing.

My favorite story of sex on the tour that directly involves me comes from the 1972 Atlanta Classic. I was preparing to putt in front of a big crowd at the eighteenth green when my concentration was interrupted by a snicker. Then several people snickered and pretty soon it sounded as though the whole gallery was falling out of the bleachers from laughter. I backed away from my ball and turned around to see what the hell they were laughing about, and there were two ducks who had come up out of the lake near the green and were furiously making love. I had to laugh and admit it was a better show than we were putting on.

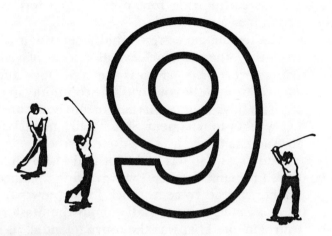

THE MASTERS

I rank the three so-called major United States tournaments this way: the Masters first, the Professional Golfers Association Championship second, the U.S. Open third. I appreciate that most fans would rank them just the reverse and so would a good many players. But I don't think any other tournament is even close to the Masters.

I can think of half a dozen reasons why I put the Masters on top. To start with the most unlikely, the Masters has more tradition. That sounds crazy, because the Masters is the youngest of the major tournaments: it started in 1934. The U.S. Open began in 1895 and the PGA in 1916. So how can the Masters have more tradition?

I don't believe in instant tradition, the kind you find in restaurants built last year with an 1890 motif, but the Masters almost produced it. The late Bobby Jones, a Georgia boy, founded the tournament and he was the most respected

81

champion in the history of golf (he had a temper as explosive as mine but learned to harness his). His idea was to gather his friends each spring for an event that was as much a class reunion as a competition.

The tournament grew rapidly because it is played earlier than the other "major" events and is played on the same course every year, whereas the U.S. Open and the PGA are moved around the country. The continuity in planning at the Masters fills a room with thick memo books and is a model for every other tournament. Smart tournament organizers travel to Augusta to see how it's done correctly.

The press also has had a lot to do with building the tradition. I remember when I was growing up, knee high to a ball washer, I read twice as much in the newspapers and heard twice as much on the radio about the Masters as any other tournament. That was the tournament all us caddies talked about and dreamed of winning some day. We knew the golf season had started when it was Masters time. Everything before that was just shadow boxing. Today more than 300 writers from all parts of the world cover the Masters. They outnumber the players at least 3 to 1. The club treats them better than other tournaments do. The press headquarters is big and has a closed-circuit television system to carry interviews with players all over the building; there are plenty of helpful officials and free food and drink. The telecasts are the most professionally done.

Mementos from the past are everywhere in the handsome white antebellum clubhouse—pictures, old equipment, souvenirs of Jones' great career. You're reminded subtly that all the great players since the mid-1930s have won the Masters: Sarazen, Nelson, Demaret, Hogan, Snead, Palmer, Player, Nicklaus. That isn't true of the other major tournaments. Snead has never won the Open and Palmer has never won the PGA, for example. But all the great ones have won at

Augusta. Monuments on the course commemorate feats like Sarazen's famous double eagle in 1935.

I love the Masters because it's a player's tournament. From the moment you check in at the front gate and drive up the tree-lined lane to the clubhouse, you are made to feel special. Everybody seems to know you, even if you're the last man in the field. The service is flawless. You never have to hunt for anything in the locker room. You can get the best steak sandwich and peaches in the world in the players' dining room. There's no hustle-bustle, but you're treated well without being fussed over and bothered.

The two practice areas are the best anywhere. The turf is good and you have plenty of room to set up shop and not be distracted by conversation from other players who are socializing or giving each other lessons. You can concentrate on working on your game. The practice areas stay open until dark. If you beat as many practice balls as I do, these are important advantages.

The caddies are local boys but they're usually good. The regular Augusta National crew is bolstered by the top caddies from other clubs in the area.

A golfer never feels crowded at Augusta. The course is spread over a vast rolling acreage and the holes are separated by trees so that each hole is a world all its own. The field is small—about 90 players as opposed to 140 or more in regular tour events—and you don't have to wait on a tee for somebody to get out of the way.

You never have to tee off before nine or ten in the morning. I don't know any golfer who likes to go to work early. I've heard a story about Walter Hagen getting an early tee time and ignoring it, something he could get away with. He said, "Hell, I don't even get up at that hour to close the window." At Augusta you're off the course by four, in time to practice if you want to and eat dinner at a sane hour and get to bed. For a guy who's supposed to be a hell-raiser, I leave a few things to be desired. On the road I'm usually asleep by 9:30 unless I find an extra-attractive card game or something to keep me awake. Golf wears me out. By the time I practice before the round, concentrate for four and a half or five hours on the course, hit balls for an hour or two, relax with a few vodka and tonics, clean up, and eat a big dinner, I'm ready for Sleep City.

At Augusta you don't have to drive a long way and fight freeway traffic to and from the golf course. Most of the players rent houses nearby. The people who own them go on vacation or move in with relatives for the week and pocket enough money to pay their taxes.

Hotel and motel space is in short supply in Augusta, which has to be the least likely setting for a major sports event. Having the Masters in Augusta is like having the Super Bowl in Joplin, Missouri, or the World Series in Salinas, California. Augusta has a population of about 75,000 and it's very much the Old South. Some parts of town are beautiful, with well-kept turn-of-the-century mansions and beautifully flowering trees and bushes. Other parts are pathetic, with ramshackle slum houses and unpaved streets and sad-looking blacks in worn-out clothes. Augusta used to be a popular resort town. It also used to be known as the home of Tobacco Road. Both sides of its reputation are still prominent.

Augusta is also an army town. Fort Gordon is nearby, and on Saturday night soldiers jam the go-go dancing parlors around town. You see many of these questionable looking massage parlors in Augusta, too. But thousands of army families retire quite respectably and quietly in Augusta for its warm climate. It's a small city of stark contrasts.

During Masters week it gets terribly overcrowded, and I'm happy to pay a thousand dollars to rent a house where I can eat and sleep in peace and be only five minutes from the course. I have fun inviting friends from all over the country to be my guests in the house, people I think will enjoy the Masters. One year I had a priest friend, a psychologist friend,

84

and a surgeon friend, and they spent the whole week analyzing me. That was good for a million laughs. They finally gave up. I like to have people around who have fun. I prefer that they play bridge and gin.

Sometimes I will be trying to reshape my game and I have a top teacher in the house. One year it was Harry Pressler from Palm Springs. Another year it was Norman Von Nida from Australia. It set me back a pretty good bundle paying for Norman's and his wife's travel expenses from Australia, but I couldn't put a price on what I learned that week. Norman is perhaps the most astute man in golf. He would follow me at the course, and at night we would go over in detail every shot I hit: the circumstances, what I was trying to achieve with the shot, why I got the results I got. Norman also is one of the last of the great raconteurs, and he kept me loose with hilarious reminiscences of making love to a woman in a bunker and chopping down a tree that interfered with a shot he was attempting to make, to give you a couple of the milder ones. Norman is even more fiery than I am. I want to tell you more about him later, because there is no one like him in golf. Or anywhere else for that matter.

Living in a roomy house and eating home-cooked food and being able to relax in the evenings with old friends beats the hell out of staring at the walls of a motel room that looks just like the motel room you stayed in last week and the week before that and the week before that. Anywhere else, I might get so relaxed under these conditions that I couldn't bring myself to a competitive pitch. Not at Augusta. The pressure causes you to breathe a little quicker and swallow a little harder all week. Lionel Hebert says it's the only tournament he knows where you choke when you drive on the grounds. There is a mystique about the Masters. I'm not much of a romantic, but Augusta National is hallowed ground to me. I see ghosts out there, ghosts of great golfers of the past, and they're watching to see how well I measure up.

If I could think of the Masters as just another golf tournament and not take it so seriously, I probably would play better. Every year about nine guys blow themselves out of contention the last day because they start thinking what a big deal it would be to win the Masters. If they could pretend it was the New Orleans Open they'd be in.

You almost have to blow this tournament to win it. Look at the players who have won the Masters for the first time in recent years. Gay Brewer folded one year and won the next. So did Bill Casper. So did Charles Coody. It's psychological more than anything else. The best chance I have had at Augusta was in 1970. The last day I birdied three out of four holes to go six under par through ten, three shots behind Littler and Casper, who were leading. I was telling myself, "This is just another tournament." Myself wasn't listening. I tied with Tommy Aaron for fifth. Littler and Casper went into a playoff that Casper won. Aaron is another who had to suffer the experience of losing the Masters before he could win it. The mystique grabs you by the throat.

It has to be the mystique. Nothing else about the tournament is particularly difficult. The field is the weakest of the year. It's small to start with, and a fifth of the players are amateurs and another fifth are foreigners. The course is littered with guys who have no chance to win. You have to beat only about 15 players instead of the usual 30.

Like the other tour players, I would like to see more American pros and fewer amateurs and foreigners that nobody has heard of. But this is one cause I'm not going to rebel for. I like the Masters so much that the makeup of the field doesn't bother me that much. I respect the right of the Augusta National Golf Club to run an invitational tournament the way it sees fit. All the invitations are based firmly on qualification categories. I think the change to invite tournament winners was an improvement. I wish it had been in effect earlier. I won two tournaments in 1961 but wasn't invited to the Masters. I first qualified in 1968 as a result of finishing high in the 1967

U.S. Open. I finished in the top 24 at Augusta in 1968 to qualify for the 1969 Masters and I'm happy to say I've been back ever since.

For years a big fuss was raised over the absence of a black tour pro in the Masters. I get tired of that talk. Contrary to what you probably have heard, the Masters never changed its rules to keep a black from qualifying. If anybody should have been given a special invitation to the Masters it is Charlie Sifford, who was barred from the tour by the PGA until he was past his prime because of one absurd reason: he was black. The men who could have invited Charlie but didn't were the past Masters champions. In 1969 and 1970 they had the right to add a man to the field. Charlie had won the Los Angeles Open in 1968. They never picked him, and you'll have to ask them why. Charlie ruffled a lot of personalities when he was fighting to make it on tour, and he wasn't bashful about telling his troubled story. That had to offend some white players. Many of the past Masters champions, especially the older ones, are from the deep South and still call a black man a "nigger." But Clifford Roberts, Bobby Jones' old associate, who ran the tournament with an iron fist in an iron glove until he retired, was happy a black, Lee Elder, finally qualified and ended the debate. And Charlie Sifford wouldn't take an invitation unless he earned it the same as everyone else.

So the field at Augusta isn't that tough. Neither is the golf course. It's a great course, but it's a 100 percent honest, fair test. Luck doesn't count for much. Skill does. Augusta National is never tricked up the way U.S. Open and PGA Championship courses are. It doesn't need any gimmicks to be a championship course. People who haven't been there are always amazed to learn there is virtually no rough at Augusta. When you don't have long grass, you eliminate a lot of luck. On many courses we play you can get a bad bounce, drive it one yard off the fairway and be in ten times more trouble than a man who slices it 25 yards off the fairway and winds up with

87

a nice lie where the fans have trampled down the rough. The man who is one yard off the fairway maybe has to take a short iron and just pitch the ball back to the fairway—what it amounts to is that he's been penalized a stroke. The man who slices the ball way off line can take a long club and go for the green. That ain't justice.

An even worse example is the typical U.S. Open course with high, heavy rough grown all around the greens. You can hit a good approach shot eight feet from the hole in the rough and you're lucky to find your ball, let alone be able to make a swing at it. But you can hit a relatively poor approach shot fifty feet from the hole and be safely on the green. That ain't justice either.

A course laid out through trees doesn't need rough. Augusta is that type of course. The trees aren't that fat or close together, but if you knock the ball far enough off line to get in them, you are going to face a challenge getting out, especially if you want to advance the ball toward the hole, which is the idea of the game. The fairways at Augusta are plenty wide, maybe twice as wide as U.S. Open fairways in the landing areas, with the exception of the short seventh hole, which is only about 40 yards wide and looks more like 10 when you're standing on the tee. You don't have much trouble driving the ball in the fairway at Augusta.

But that's deceptive. Player after player fails to score well at Augusta because he doesn't think well enough on the tee. You have to position your tee shot carefully to set up a good second shot. Augusta is a second shot golf course. You have to get your second shot close to the hole to have a reasonable chance to 2-putt. And to ensure yourself a good second shot you have to make a pinpoint drive even if you're looking at a big, wide-open fairway with no trouble in sight. That takes concentration and planning. At Augusta you plan your strategy on a hole backward from the cup because the greens are the hardest part of the course. The greens *are* the course.

They're the old hand-built variety with a million cleverly constructed contours, and they are faster than a fart in a hot skillet. Ordinarily the pros prefer fast greens. Average players are afraid of them, but we are just the opposite. The ball doesn't break as much on fast greens, you don't have to put a knockout punch on it, and you concentrate better. But Augusta's greens are faster than fast. I like Sam Snead's line. He says the greens in the Masters are so fast he hollers "Whoa!" before he hits a putt. The greens are a combination of four grasses and are extra fast because they're top-dressed in the fall. During the tournament they play entirely differently than they do the rest of the year because they are mowed twice a day until they're almost scalped. They actually get faster and faster while you're playing. In one hour in the morning they get twice as fast, as the dew dries and the wind comes up. You have to be fantastically careful with every putt and never get the ball above the hole where you'll be left with a downhill putt. If you try to force a birdie, you'll get a bogey —or worse. It's absurdly easy to 3-putt from twelve feet. One year Larry Hinson 4-putted from eight feet—and he's a good putter!

The cup positions don't help at all. Often the hole will be cut on top of a knoll. You have to roll the ball uphill to the hole, but if you go past the hole the ball will take off as if somebody kicked it. You can't see the subtle breaks close to the hole on television. Sometimes you can't see them if you're a pro lining up a six-footer either. The caddiemaster doesn't even know all the breaks in the Masters greens. I have more trouble reading the direction of the grain at Augusta than anywhere else. The local smart guys will tell you it breaks toward Rae's Creek, but I can't find a pattern in it. Many times I'll misread the grain and find out too late that it runs exactly opposite of what I thought. The best policy at Augusta is to hit a putt straight and firmly. And pray a lot.

The course definitely favors players like Nicklaus, Weiskopf, and Ray Floyd who putt well on fast greens and hit long, high tee balls and irons. Trevino has talked himself into thinking he can't play well at Augusta because he hits the ball too low. He's exaggerating (he also believes he is looked down on at Augusta because he's Mexican, and I can't say about that, although I've seen no evidence of it), but it is true that if you don't drive the ball high at Augusta you can lose considerable distance landing into fairway mounds, and if you don't hit your irons high you have trouble stopping the ball near the hole on those firm greens. The course couldn't have been designed any better to suit Nicklaus' game if he'd done the job himself. He ought to be fined every time he fails to win the Masters.

Arnold Palmer has played brilliantly at Augusta over the years. He mastered the greens when he was in his prime, and the crowds down there still pick him up. "Arnie's Army" first marched at the Masters in the early 1960s. He had charisma plus he was a golfing pal of General Eisenhower, who played at Augusta National.

Arnold is a favorite son of the tournament management. He always gets the benefit of the doubt if he's involved in a questionable rules interpretation. At Augusta there's one set of rules for Palmer and another set for everybody else. Palmer isn't breaking the rules on purpose, but he presses for every advantage he can get, and at Augusta he gets one after another. On the tour, players are paired by formula to avoid favoritism. The Masters pairs arbitrarily. You know Palmer is going to get an outstanding pairing. You'll never see him going off really early or late, or playing with a slow player or somebody who is liable to distract him.

I think the Masters likes to pair the "bad guys" together. I'll be paired with Raymond Floyd, for example. Maybe they're having a little fun for the fans' sake. That's okay with me. Raymond and I enjoy each other's company. But I guess now that Raymond's won it I'll have to get another partner.

But the tournament brass will stop at nothing to keep Palmer happy. There is a story that he left the eleventh fairway one year to go into the woods and relieve himself. The next year a permanent restroom had been built on the spot.

The fans love him in Augusta. To them he's still the man to beat, even if several dozen players are beating him. I won't knock the Augusta fans, though. They appreciate good golf and are probably the best behaved we see. The Masters is the easiest tournament to gallery. There is plenty of room to walk, big mounds have been built for better viewing, scoreboards are plentiful and kept up to the minute through an underground telephone cable system. Feature pairings are spread out so the fans can move from one group to another.

Large grandstands have been built at several key holes, and thousands of fans stay in one comfortable spot and watch the entire field come through. A good spot is behind the tee on the short, treacherous twelfth hole. From there you also can see the eleventh green and thirteenth tee. Some of the fans at the twelfth have been coming there for years. I met a couple from Iowa that was vacationing at the twelfth hole for the twentieth straight year. Another good spot is the large grandstand alongside the green on the par-5 fifteenth. The fans like to see whether the players will go for the green with long second shots, braving a pond. They can look over and see the short sixteenth hole too. To the left of the water on 16 you get a congregation of teeny-boppers every year. They aren't always paying that much attention to the golf, but they're having fun. There is a lot of good spectating space and a large stand built up around the eighteenth green, and on the last day it's one of the most dramatic settings in sports.

The Masters refuses to announce attendance figures. Clifford Roberts hinted in the past that the daily crowds run about 30,000. I'm going to guess that almost twice that many are on the grounds every day of the tournament. The grounds are so spacious, and there are so many good vantage points, you never get an idea of how many people are spread out across the course. Only season badges are sold, and they're taken years in advance.

Mr. Roberts, as he's commonly called, was the main brains and energy behind the Masters. He's a semi-retired Wall Street investment banker who discovered the site, suggested the idea of a tournament to his friend Bobby Jones, and named it the Masters. He ran it with an absolute obsession for detail. Every year dozens of little changes are made in the course and the conduct of the tournament to improve it. Roberts' crisp memos laid end to end would reach to St. Andrews in Scotland.

I wonder what will happen to the Masters now that Roberts has retired. Something already went out of the Masters when Jones died. Since then some of the past champions stopped coming for their annual dinner, notably the Texas Mafia —Hogan, Demaret, Burke. Hogan once had a run-in on the course with Roberts, one of the few men ever to try to tell Ben how to play. Roberts ordered Hogan to speed up. Hogan told Roberts to stick it, give or take a couple of hard-bitten words.

Roberts insisted on doing so much himself that he didn't delegate enough authority to develop a strong successor. Billy Joe Patton was rumored to be in line for Roberts' job a few years ago, but he got crossways with Roberts when he spoke out on something or other, and Roberts drummed him clear out of the club. I suspect the firm hand of Mr. Roberts will continue to be very much in evidence.

I don't believe the Masters ever will be anything less than a great tournament. Too much thorough groundwork has been laid over too many years for it to go downhill very far. It's still in a class all its own. It's the only truly major tournament we have.

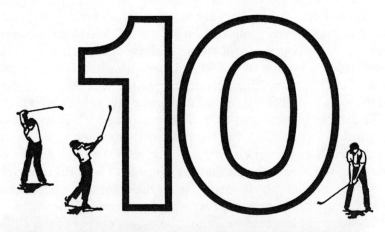

THE OTHER TOURNAMENTS

The PGA Championship should be the best tournament in the world. Should be but isn't.

It has the best field of the four "major" tournaments. You don't have a lot of amateurs getting in the way, gathering stories to tell their grandchildren about the time they played against the big pros, the way you do in the Masters and U.S. Open. The British Open never draws a strong enough group of Americans because of the travel and the comparatively primitive conditions.

The PGA Championship used to take in too many club pros. A few of them could play—guys like Jimmy Wright and Terry Wilcox and Jerry Pittman—but they were all former tour players. Most of them either never had enough talent to play against the tour pros or had worked with so many bad swings on the lesson tee that their own swings went to hell. The PGA finally started a separate national tournament for the club pros in order to give the tour players more spots in the main championship, and now the PGA Championship probably gets every player who has a chance to win, which is how it should have been all along.

I know I take pride in trying to be the best at my game, and the place to prove it should be in the PGA Championship against all my peers. Unfortunately, some of the other players don't think so much of the PGA Championship, for political reasons. They're holding grudges over the feud between the players and the PGA national officers a few years ago which split the organization in half. There is too much petty background to go into here, but the players threatened to walk out of the PGA and start their own tour, and they did wind up forming the Tournament Players Division. The TPD is under the PGA banner but in reality is an independent operation, with its own Tournament Players Championship now.

I have never been excited about being a member of the TPD and was one of the few players who stuck by the PGA during the dispute. I grew up with the sole aim in life of being a professional golfer, which meant being a member of the PGA. I have worked as a club pro and still do at the course I lease in Denver. I maintain the old-fashioned view that you aren't a full-fledged golf pro unless you can play well and also give a lesson to a 95 shooter and repair a club and interpret the rulebook.

The new generation on the tour comes out of college; they know nothing about the game except how to shoot pars and open bank accounts, and wouldn't know a loft and lie machine if they tripped over one. These guys want their own championship that would displace the PGA Championship as a major tournament. I oppose the idea in principle and in practice.

Don't get the idea I'm a booster of the PGA officers, because I never have been. They're mainly just a bunch of glorified caddies. They are old establishment types who haven't had a new idea in ten years. They love playing amateur politics but do almost nothing for their 7,000 members. They don't give the young club pro good understanding of how to teach or how to merchandise. The pro shop is about to be run out of business by department stores and discount houses, and the PGA people will be the last ones to realize it. The PGA is your typical association—not worth much except its fancy letterhead stationery.

When the players set up their own division of the PGA and virtually stopped talking to the PGA officers down in South Florida, they took with them everything that meant anything in pro golf except the Ryder Cup and the PGA Championship. The PGA brass still has those two opportunities to strut around at an important event. We call them the Red Jackets. They're all over the place looking extremely official but doing mostly nothing.

They hire Ed Carter, an independent operator, to run the PGA Championship; otherwise it would be a shambles. Even so, you never can find a scoreboard to find out what's happening. And to show you how smart the PGA is, Carter talked them into letting him sell the ads for the tournament program and makes upward of $100,000 a year on it for himself. That's money that could be going into the PGA's coffers.

The PGA Championship has been held back more than anything else by poor selection of golf courses. We have played our premier tournament on some real dog tracks. The low point was in 1968 at Pecan Valley Country Club in San Antonio. That was a perfect illustration of how the PGA officers can play politics at the expense of their championship. Warren Cantrell was a past president of the PGA. Warren Cantrell also was a member and prime mover in Pecan Valley and reportedly very close to the people who were developing the real estate around it. While Warren Cantrell was president of the PGA he saw to it that the PGA Championship was awarded to Pecan Valley. By the time the tournament rolled around,

95

Cantrell had been out of office for some time and nobody could imagine how the PGA selected such a mediocre course.

And that's being too flattering. The eighteenth hole, the finishing hole for a major championship, mind you, was a layup par-4—you laid up off the tee! Your second shot was a 3-wood to a green built for a middle-iron approach shot. I'd rather not discuss the first seventeen holes.

In recent years the PGA has been picking better courses. We had the National Cash Register course in Dayton in 1969, Southern Hills in Tulsa in 1970, PGA National in Palm Beach in 1971, Oakland Hills near Detroit in 1972, and Canterbury near Cleveland in 1973, all splendid courses. Tanglewood in North Carolina in 1974, Firestone in 1975, and Congressional in 1976 aren't in that league, but happily they're no Pecan Valley either.

Some of the players are talking up a permanent site for the PGA Championship. I feel that the PGA is a national championship and it should be moved around the country. But only to great courses. Then the tournament's image will improve, and it will challenge for No. 1 ranking. The press will jump on the bandwagon and help promote it. You have to have the press brainwashing people for you to do much good.

The press likes to write that the PGA committed suicide when it changed its championship from match play to medal play after the 1957 tournament. (Oddly, Lionel Hebert beat Dow Finsterwald in the finals of the last match-play tournament and the next year Finsterwald won the first stoke-play tournament.) The press blames television for the demise of match play.

I don't blame the death of match play—if it is dead—on television except as a party of the second part. From what I've heard, television never went to golf and said, "Okay, either you play the PGA Championship at medal play or we're not going to televise it." I don't doubt that television prefers medal play, but I think golf badly wants the big money from televi-

96

sion and does what it figures will please television. That isn't television's fault. Blaming television would be like blaming a cow for giving milk that a farmer goes out and sells at inflated prices.

Match play can be exciting, with the head-to-head action and all the psychology and strategy that go with it. But medal play is a fairer test. Seventy-two-hole tournaments may get tiresome, but they're the best way to decide a champion. Match play leaves room for too many flukes. I'd like to see match play stay alive in golf, but not in a major championship.

The fans lose interest in a match-play tournament if you don't get at least one big name into the finals. Look what happened to the L & M Tournament in North Carolina. It died after two years because DeWitt Weaver and John Schroeder won it. Nobody came to watch the tournament, and the television audiences found something else to do.

Another distinctive feature of the PGA Championship used to be that the winner got a lifetime exemption to play in tour events, including the PGA Championship. They finally put a stop to that a few years ago, but they didn't go far enough: they didn't make it retroactive. It was a nice incentive to win the tournament, but we shouldn't need that type of incentive to win our own championship. The result of the exemption is that you are still finding old fellows like Jim Ferrier and Doug Ford and Jerry Barber coming out and playing. They take a vacation and go play in a golf tournament. They seldom make the cut and they take up a spot in the field at a big tournament like Westchester that ought to go to a young pro who's trying to make himself a future. These old guys ought to realize they can't play well enough anymore and get out of the way of the young guys. In their day they were good, but their day is gone. They should know the old has to make room for the new. Charles Darwin said that, I believe, although he never played in the PGA Championship. These old-timers ought to take a clue from Jay Hebert. He won the PGA but has never taken advantage of it. He has his lifetime exemption, but when he got to where he couldn't beat people he retired gracefully and got married and has been living sanely ever after.

Today the PGA champion is exempt for ten years, which still is twice too long. Five years should be the maximum exemption for anything. I remember it was funny when the rule was changed from a lifetime exemption to a ten-year exemption: Dave Stockton was one of the young players who had been lobbying loudly in favor of the change. He always kidded his pal Al Geiberger, who had won the 1965 PGA, that Al didn't deserve that kind of a free ride. So who was the first player to get caught by the change? Stockton, who won at Tulsa in 1970. A ten-year exemption is still a helluva prize for a younger pro. That knocks off a lot of pressure.

I've played well in the PGA just once, at Palm Beach in 1971. That was the year the tournament was held first instead of last. It was in the winter, and I play better early in the year. I run out of juice later on. I got off to a slow start at Palm Beach, shooting a 74, but then went 71-71-70 for a 2-under-par 286 that tied for sixth as Jack Nicklaus became the first man to win two PGAs at medal play, with 281. I suppose if I'd won it that year, I'd call the PGA the best tournament there is. As it is, I'm being more honest and saying it soon should be.

Behind the PGA I put the U.S. Open, the most overrated tournament in the universe. The U.S. Open is just another tournament, except that the course is tricked up. The United States Golf Association, which sponsors the tournament, does a great job of picking courses, with a few hideous exceptions like Hazeltine, but then turns around and ruins them. It's perverse.

I couldn't believe what the USGA did to Pebble Beach, a classic test. I barely recognized it. Pebble is one of my favorite courses on the tour—but the USGA turned a show dog into a bitch. I played out the tournament at Pebble and wished I hadn't.

Left: Tour commissioner Deane Beman and I seem to be agreeing—this time. *(Steve Deal)*
Below: My long-time caddy Junior helps me prepare before a tournament. *(Steve Deal)*

Finding out which way they're moving today. *(Steve Deal)*

← This is a practice bunker. The cigarette
is usually missing when the chips are
down. *(Steve Deal)*

This ball is going to fade in over the bunker right to the flag. *(Bill Mount)*

Checking scorecard after the round. *(Bill Mount)* ➤

Three-hour work session on green with Mike helped him
take tour first at Doral. *(Lester Nehamkin)*

Tom Weiskopf on way to the first tee. ➤
(Columbus Dispatch)

Jack lines up a long slider. *(David L. Oshin)*

If you don't recognize this guy, you haven't been watching. *(Will Hertzberg)*

Young Ben Crenshaw might be one of the tour greats very soon. *(Golf Digest)*

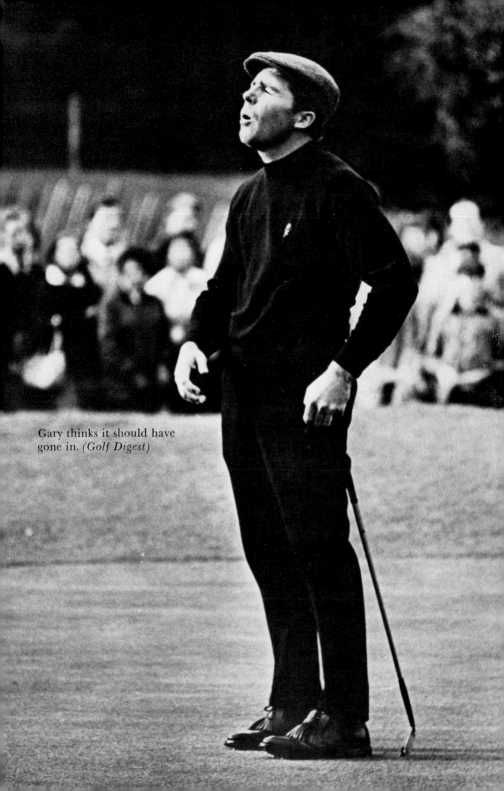

Gary thinks it should have gone in. *(Golf Digest)*

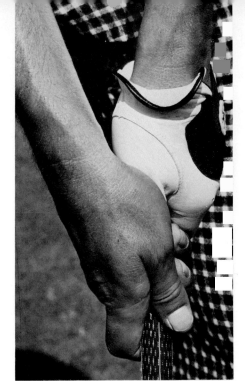

The grip has got to be right.
(Golf Digest)

← It went in *(David L. Oshin)*

Swing sequence—full swing with 3-iron. Note the quick wrist set and leg action through the ball. *(Leonard Kamsler)*

My most faithful fan, Sandie. She walks almost every hole with me. *(AAR Photos)*

I like the way they're flying during the pre-round practice at Memphis. *(Memphis Press-Scimitar)*

→Junior helps me line up putt. This action caused a lot of heat on the tour. *(Lester Nehamkin)*

This kid, Pate, has a fine swing and a winning attitude. *(Bill Mount)*

A pair of good ole boys: Hubie Green and Ray Floyd. *(Tony Roberts)*

The next year I went to Oakmont on the assumption that here was a course that definitely needed no doctoring . . . no knee-high rough and cement-hard greens. Naive me. I played four holes of a practice round and checked it to 'em. I went home. I didn't pick any fights or throw anything in the locker room or even criticize the USGA. The writers grilled me and I held my tongue. I simply went home. I wasn't mentally prepared to go out there and shoot 80, and that's what I would have done. There's no law that says I can't quit, and I quit. My swing had been coming along and my attitude was good and I didn't want to ruin them both. I couldn't have won the golf tournament if they'd given me a free throw on every hole. I paid my caddie $150 for the four holes and took off.

I'm a skinny little cat who has to win with style, not strength, and the game is no fun at all for me when a course is prepared like that. I don't understand it. It doesn't happen in the big events in other major sports. They don't dig chuck holes in the track for the Indianapolis 500. They don't move the goalposts back into the crowd in the Super Bowl. They don't put obstacles on the center court at Forest Hills. They play the game the same way it's played the rest of the season. They're content to let the best man win under normal conditions, and he will.

Not the almighty USGA. The USGA could screw up "Hello." It's made up of a bunch of "little old ladies" with a warped idea of tradition. They think they're the inheritors of all the blue blood in the game, and they're in all their old-school-tie glory when the Open comes around once a year. That's when the last of the old-fashioned amateurs can show up the pros. They love it.

I don't object to anything about the Open except the setting up of the course. It's wonderful that the national championship is open to everybody who can play his way in. The tournament is pretty efficiently run, but the USGA makes the course almost unplayable.

You always hear about the heavy rough pinching the fairways, but in the Open it's around the greens where you lose the most strokes. The USGA grows rough where the fringe grass ordinarily would be. The fairway rough is bad enough. You can be three feet off the fairway and have to give up a stroke; you might just as well be out of bounds. You often have no chance to go for the green on a par-4 hole—you can't do anything but chop the ball sideways back to the fairway. That's humiliating enough, but then around the greens you have a whole new ball game.

You can be barely off the green, hole-high, and virtually have an unplayable lie. You won't be able to find your ball and you tramp around terrified that you're going to step on it and cost yourself a penalty stroke. In effect, you're liable to get a penalty stroke for missing the green anyway, because you can't do anything with the recovery shot but jab at it. Chipping is eliminated, although I've always considered chipping a delicate and important part of the game.

Growing rough right up to the green can be very unfair. It means that one player can be 15 feet from the hole and be in deep grass with almost no shot to play and another player can be 45 feet from the hole with a comparatively easy shot. The USGA likes to get the greens as hard as a sidewalk, and you can hit a good approach shot and have no chance to hold the green. You go in the deep grass with absolutely no chance to make par. I've never figured out how to play that shot. I usually stand around and guess a lot. Some players use a sand wedge and try to explode the ball as if they were in a bunker, but that doesn't work for me. You only have the shot once a year and it's hard to adjust.

It could be smarter for you to hit the ball into a greenside bunker and explode with a sand wedge from there. Gary Player, the best bunker player in the world, actually aims approach shots into bunkers on some holes in the U.S. Open and counts on getting up and down in two shots.

I know the USGA's theory behind tricking up the Open courses. They believe that conditions in the national championship should be the same from year to year. Back around the turn of the century some sadist decided that the U.S. Open ought to bring all the players to their knees, so it's been that way ever since. Scrambling is supposed to be taboo. Low scores would be an embarrassment to the grand old USGA. Let them make bogeys! So be it.

The USGA isn't going to change and neither am I. The way I feel today, I'll never play in another U.S. Open. I don't need that kind of aggravation. The USGA won't miss me.

Unbeknownst to many casual golf fans, the USGA does much more than stage the Open once a year. The Old School Ties also set the rules of the game, fix the definitions of amateurism, and control the development of the equipment we play with. It does these things diligently and quietly. Maybe too diligently and quietly.

Somebody has to oversee these standards, and if the USGA didn't do it, I don't know who would. The tour easily could come up with a more sensible rulebook for itself, but who would look out for the 16 million amateur golfers? I am a fastidious advocate of playing by the rules, but the rulebook has become so ridiculously long and complex that nobody understands it, not even the top players. We've forgotten that the game once was played with only one rule: you hit the ball from tee to hole without touching it. Very simple. We need to move back to simplicity in the rules.

The USGA is living in the nineteenth century with its absurd definitions of amateur status. A college golfer in this day and age is as much a pro as I am. He's taking at least four years of education free, which is worth probably $20,000, and he's probably getting plenty more under the table. But the USGA classifies him as an amateur, the same as a weekend player who can accept no more than $250 worth of merchandise as a tournament prize.

101

The USGA is getting more aggressive in its policing of equipment trends that promise greater distance for all players, understandably worrying that the character of the game, the length of courses, and the records made over the years suddenly could be made obsolete. The USGA doesn't communicate well with the manufacturers, though, and one of these days the manufacturers are liable to band together and take the USGA to court over some of its high-handed edicts—and I'm going to lay money on the manufacturers. The USGA tried to ram a compromise ball size down everybody's throats—mainly for the sake of worldwide uniformity—and the manufacturers, who would have had to spend fortunes to regear their ball-making machinery, re-belled. The USGA finally gave up and announced that the project was being delayed for "further study." It's dead.

For all its Eastern-establishment stuffiness and failure to keep up with the times, I have to admit the USGA is necessary. If it didn't exist, we would have to create something like it. If we could just get the people over there to join the twentieth century . . .

As far as the other so-called major tournament, the British Open, I don't play in it because the conditions are primitive, including most of the golf courses. In Britain, nature builds the courses, not man. You're liable to find the worst trouble on a hole in the middle of the fairway, where I've always been taught you are supposed to drive the ball. If you don't like a course, you don't play as well. The idea is to play the game for fun, and if it isn't fun why play?

It's a long trip for one tournament and you have to file your entry too early.

The weather is usually abysmal. If the temperature reaches 55 degrees over there they think they're having a heat wave. The wind roars in off the ocean on those links courses and the rain lashes you, and you bundle up to survive and you can't make a decent golf swing. They play faster over there and it's

102

no wonder—if you don't keep moving you're liable to turn into an icicle.

The weather is why the British pros for years couldn't hit the ball anywhere. They couldn't make a full swing, so they manipulated the ball with their hands. They would come over to this country and they couldn't beat Andy Gump until they'd been here five years.

I appreciate the traditions of the game but I don't have any warm spot in my heart for Britain. As far as I'm concerned we've refined the game tremendously over here and I don't get any thrills out of going back and roughing it. Give me running water every time.

Those folks are about 200 years behind America in modernization, you know. Especially out where some of these seaside golf links are. At the '69 Ryder Cup we were in a hotel that has something like 120 rooms, and out of those 120 rooms there are 27 private bathrooms. I was lucky—I had a private bath. Otherwise I would have used the window before I'd have headed down the hallway at 4 A.M. And that is one of the luxury hotels in the area!

The British Open is the oldest big tournament, but I don't even classify it as a major event today. The British Open probably would have died if the American stars hadn't started going over to play in it more regularly the last 15 years. Arnold Palmer saved it, but as far as I'm concerned he didn't do us any favors.

ARCHITECTURE

I called a U.S. Open course a cow pasture a few years ago, which was an accurate description, and I've been known ever since as the world's most hateful critic of courses and course architects. As soon as I hit town the local writers ask me what I think of the course, hoping I'll say something controversial so they can turn out some juicy stories. Joe Finger, a Texas golf architect, jumps all over me and says I knock courses I can't play well with no regard for their merits. I'm getting the Finger unjustly.

Let me explain what happened at the U.S. Open at Hazeltine Golf Club in Chaska, Minnesota, in 1970. I went to Minnesota from Denver with an old friend, Bell Wallen. Bell is a retired ladies' ready-to-wear apparel man who lived near me in Evergreen, Colorado, and helps me run a municipal course we lease in Denver. It was Bell who locked my clubs in his garage after the 1968 season and convinced me to relax and get away from the game for several weeks. He probably saved

104

me a nervous breakdown. He also had a great deal to do with my having the best year of my career in 1969.

Anyway, Bell and I flew in to the Minneapolis airport on Monday for the U.S. Open and got a car for the 40-mile drive to Chaska. We had detailed directions but got severely lost. After an hour and a half of driving around in the outback, we still hadn't found Chaska and no one we stopped to ask had ever heard of it. We began to wonder if we were in the right state. Finally we stumbled onto beautiful downtown Chaska and I could see why we'd been lost. It consisted of a country store and a filling station with old-fashioned hand-operated gasoline pumps that had the gas up above. Fittingly enough, there was a Model-T parked nearby.

We went to the course and I played nine holes and quit. I had time to play nine more but I couldn't stand the course. I loved beautiful downtown Chaska by comparison. I had never seen a nine with so many hidden driving areas. You had no target to shoot at. On the first hole, you aimed at a silo, but the silo was a mile away on a hill and that isn't much help when you're trying to judge the distance. I tried to aim at a cow on a couple of other holes. That worked if the cow didn't move. A fairway would dogleg to the left but fall off to the right. That's about as logical as driving your car down the road and signaling for a left turn and then going right. From the tee, you couldn't tell where the rough line left off and the fairway started. You would just hit a drive and watch it disappear. It's like taking a friend out to your course for the first time, and he hits what he thinks is a great drive and then you say, "Well, that's okay, but it went in the water." That's the type of course Hazeltine is.

I came in and told Bell we were going back to Denver, immediately. He talked me out of it over a few drinks—the best time to talk me out of drastic moves—and the next day, Tuesday, I played the back nine and quit again. I had figured no U.S. Open course could have two nines that were that atrocious, but I was wrong. There were more blind shots. The greens resembled Indian burial mounds more than anything else. And their horses had been buried along with the Indians. I hit balls on the practice range for the rest of the day and kept asking myself how the United States Golf Association in its infinite wisdom could pick such a dog of a course for its premier championship. Hazeltine has to be the worst course ever to play host to an Open. I later learned that Tot Heffelfinger, the president of Hazeltine, is a former USGA president. He had planned a real estate development around the golf club out there in the sticks and obviously used his political leverage with the USGA to get the Open as a promotional tool. That's the first time I heard the USGA was in the real estate business instead of the golf business. Hopefully it will be the last.

Every other pro I talked to that week was just as disgusted with the course as I was, although you never read their opinions, only mine. I'm sure I could have been more discreet in my remarks to the press. A lot of nice people volunteered a lot of their time at Hazeltine to produce the best tournament they could for players like me. I make a rich living because of people like that. I meant no slam at them or their club. But when reporters asked me what I thought of the course I had no thought except to answer their questions. I never said anything at Hazeltine that wasn't an answer to a newsman's question, and for that I was crucified.

The first day of the tournament was uneventful. I shot a 75 and nobody was looking to interview me. The next day I shot 69 and they wanted me in the pressroom. I was in a bad mood from fighting that damned course—you'd have to play it four or five times to have any idea where to hit the ball on many holes—and I said I didn't want to go. I chugged down four vodka and tonics on an empty stomach and was feeling no pain when they asked me again, and I went. The first questioner asked me how I found the course. My mind flashed

106

back to that first day in town when Bell and I literally couldn't find the damn place and I replied, "I'm still looking for it." Somebody asked me what I thought of the course and I said I thought Mr. Jones (Robert Trent Jones, the course designer) ruined a beautiful piece of farmland. At this point, I was still serious. I'm a farm boy and I know a good piece of farmland when I see one. I really thought Mr. Jones had ruined what could have been a fine farm.

But all the writers were laughing and having a good time and now I joined in, the four vodka and tonics not holding me back. In answer to a question about the greens, I said I thought Mr. Jones' foreman got the blueprint turned upside down when he built the greens. Another writer asked me what I thought the course needed and I said 80 acres of corn and a few cows. I borrowed that crack from Bob Rosburg.

It went from bad to worse. I was joking and had my tongue in my cheek so far it was about to poke through the side of my face. I enjoy kidding people and can take kidding pretty well myself. But when those newspaper stories came out you would have thought I said everything with great bitterness toward Jones and the tournament people. It was a slow week for the writers and they turned me into a big story. I got more ink making wisecracks about the course than I could have got winning the tournament.

If nothing else, I had a barrel of laughs that week. The galleries gave me the business about farmland and cows and I gave it back to them and it was mostly in good fun. Another friend from Denver, Doc Dean, had arrived and he's always good for my sense of humor. Doc is my gynecologist—I'm his only male patient and the only guy I know on the tour with a gynecologist. Actually he was my first wife's gynecologist, but I go to him whenever there's anything wrong with me and he sends me to an appropriate specialist. I played pretty well the last three days and Doc and I plotted a little prank in case I won. A farmer lived right across the street from the club and had a big John Deere tractor with a big plow in his front yard. Doc and I had paid the farmer $50 to let us use his tractor if I won. I was going to drive out on the course on it holding up the trophy for kicks. Tony Jacklin won going away and I was second, so the farmer made an easy 50 bucks.

After I had played on Sunday, a lady who seemed quite charming and pleasant approached me and said, "Congratulations. I am Mrs. Trent Jones." I said, "It's nice to meet you ma'am," and kept going because I figured she might be tempted to kill me if I gave in to the urge to chuckle. I have never sat down and talked with Mr. Jones—I understand he is an interesting, friendly man—but if I did visit with him I would have to tell him I don't think much of his courses, the ones I have played. I think the man must hate golfers. I think he was a pretty good player when he was younger, but I'll bet he doesn't play much nowadays. I'd like to see him have to break 90 for a living on some of these monsters he designs.

Spyglass on the Monterey Peninsula in California, one of the courses for the Bing Crosby Tournament, is another abortion by Jones. That's a magnificent stretch of property, some of the prettiest scenery in the world, and the golf course is a disaster area. Given what the man had to work with, it's awful. Spyglass is too difficult for anyone to play enjoyably. The pros hate it and maybe Jones will say we're just red-eared because we can't break par. Well, how about the poor 12-handicappers who go out there and pay $20 and shoot 120? That's sure to bring you back tomorrow. If you choose to play that course two days in a row, you have to be a masochist.

I have to believe that Mr. Jones, with his big reputation, has designed some good golf courses. I just don't happen to have seen any of them. His basic philosophy seems to be that a course must be ten miles long and almost impossibly difficult or else he is going to look bad. Some of his tees are longer than airport landing strips and don't even point in the right direction. He gives you virtually no chance to get out of a fairway bunker. I'll admit that he has the reputation and is in demand all over the world. That may be one reason he doesn't build better courses. He must take on a hundred projects a year and he can't possibly give enough personal attention to any of them. Course design is much more than blueprints on drawing boards. A good architect has to stay in close touch with a course while it's being built. It's a very delicate, personal, involved job giving birth to a golf course, and I don't see how Mr. Jones can devote enough time to a course to make it great.

Because my comments about Mr. Jones and Hazeltine got such wide circulation, people assume that I never have anything good to say about any course or any architect. That bugs me. I have as many favorites as the next fellow, only nobody ever quotes me when I say something flattering. News has to be negative to travel fast. I think Cypress Point and Pebble Beach, near Spyglass on the Monterey Peninsula, are great courses. They're beautiful, they aren't horrendously long, and they're shotmakers' courses. There are a lot of golf courses I like. Champions in Houston has two outstanding courses. Whitemarsh in Philadelphia is a fine test. So is Merion just outside Philadelphia. I love Augusta National. Oakland Hills in Michigan is a great course. I like just about all the courses I play on the tour; that's because I tend to play in tournaments because of the courses.

Over all, I'd have to pick Pebble Beach as the greatest test of golf in America. It isn't backbreakingly long—it's well under 7,000 yards from the back tees—but it demands one good shot after another. There are no shortcuts. Often you will hit every club in your bag in eighteen holes. The greens are small, and when the wind dries them out they are awfully hard to hold, even with short-iron shots. The course is on the ocean and the winds can change the character of the course suddenly and repeatedly. Jimmy Demaret has said that if you moved Pebble Beach 50 miles inland, no one would ever have heard of it. That's one of the rare dumb things I've heard from Demaret.

It's like saying if Sophia Loren weren't a girl, she wouldn't be a sexy actress. Pebble has a terrific stretch of finishing holes, capped by the famous eighteenth, a par-5 winding along the cliff top overlooking the ocean. The secret of Pebble, so obvious it often isn't noticed, is its naturalness. Nothing about it is gimmicky or forced. It appears simply to have grown spectacularly out of the setting God gave it, and yet it's tough enough that no one can humble it. Maybe the fact that the architect, Jack Neville, was an amateur is significant.

Among the modern architects, I rank George Fazio at the top. He doesn't do many courses, but the ones he does are young classics. He did a course in Florida near Palm Beach called Jupiter Hills that is the most imaginatively designed course I've seen in a long time. There is a trend in modern architecture to copy the famous old British courses, sometimes right down to the last bunker. Now that really takes a lot of creativity. I wish we could get some refreshing new design for a change. Fazio is making breakthroughs in his thinking. Jupiter Hills looks like anything but one of those typically flat-chested, boring Florida layouts. It has elevations up to 70 feet. To give the course variety in looks and strategy, he has set up multiple teeing areas, as many as five on a hole. You usually don't see any tee except the one you're on, and the hole looks and plays strikingly different from one tee to the next. Fazio backed up the tees on the par-3 eleventh and fourteenth holes, so you're sure to have a good test with the breeze behind you on one and against you on the other. Laying out the sixteenth hole, George couldn't decide between two terrific sites for the green, one of them on top of a dune—so he built two greens. He's a genius with little twists like these that make a course memorable.

I was first attracted to Fazio's work by the Jackrabbit Course at Champions Golf Club in Houston. The other Champions course, Cypress Creek, gets all the attention. That's where the Houston Open used to be played and where Orville Moody (you remember Orville Moody) won the 1969 U.S. Open. But I've always thought Jackrabbit is an even better course than Cypress. It's not as long, but more demanding. You can't get away with anything driving the ball, or on your second shot either. We play too many courses on the tour that are drive-and-putt courses. They eliminate all-around shotmaking. Jackrabbit demands it. The only course of Fazio's I don't like is Butler National, where we play the Western Open. It's too long and tough even for our biggest hitters, let alone me.

Pete Dye is another modern architect whose work I enjoy, what I've seen of it. He's done a fascinating job of combining the classic with the modern. At the Harbour Town course on Hilton Head Island he did some of the most striking par-3 holes you can imagine, using old railroad ties to build up a green or bunker, for example. He did a course in the Dominican Republic called La Romana which I haven't seen, but I understand it's another singular job.

I can't keep up with all the new courses supposedly being designed at least in part by tour players. Everybody in the top 60 seems to be in the course design business on the side. I can't believe very many of the players—if any—have the time and energy to work hard at it. Bruce Devlin appears to, but then his golf game has gone to hell in a hatbox the last few years. Player, Palmer, Nicklaus—they're all designing courses, mostly for resorts. That's where the new courses are being built, there and in the middle of real estate developments.

Nicklaus takes architecture seriously. He has always been highly thoughtful about course design and is giving more and more of his time to it, building courses as far away as Japan. He and Pete Dye used to be partners, but Pete got tired of everybody thinking Jack did all the clever designing when Jack's role probably wasn't that big. Jack has done a course in his home town of Palm Beach, called Myacoo, that has some really solid and intriguing use of water from tee to green and that makes good use of the scenic countryside. I understand

111

his Muirfield Village course in Ohio is sensational. I'm sure he can be good at any aspect of the golf business he wants to apply himself toward, and I wouldn't be surprised if he becomes a tremendous designer. The profession could certainly use him.

Okay, Hill, if you're so damned smart, why don't you design the ultimate golf course? I can hear the question rattling around between your ears. I don't design courses right now because it's all I can do to play golf and still keep my head on straight. I'll be the first to tell you I could not start from scratch and design and build a golf course. I wouldn't know how to plot the drainage, for one thing, and drainage may be the most important feature of the course, even though you don't think about it until it rains six inches. You can't afford to have water standing in the middle of a fairway or green. I am confident I could design a good golf course. I know what I would want in an ideal course, and it doesn't jibe with what most of today's architects are doing.

For openers, I know a couple of prominent trends I would avoid. Golf courses are being built for the touring pro when they should be built for the member. The touring pro comes to town once a year, if at all, and then he's gone. The member has to play the course all year. He pays the bills. No course should measure more than 6,700 yards unless it's in high altitudes in someplace like Colorado or New Mexico. These 7,400-yard courses are a waste of valuable real estate. People think good players will tear up a shorter course, but what happens when the best pros tackle a well-designed little course like Merion? The winner is lucky to shoot par. So what if he shot 250? The fans like to see the pros make birdies. Long courses can be a great excuse for top-of-the-head design.

You can't tell me a member enjoys playing a course over 7,000 yards long unless he also enjoys letting his enemies kick him in the shins with combat boots. Golf is a game, and it's no fun if you have to strain to drive the ball farther than you

112

know how on every hole, hitting drivers on 230-yard par-3 holes and 3-wood second shots short of the green on the par-4s. You have enough in your everyday life to upset you, and when you go to the golf course you don't want to be frustrated all afternoon.

Golf is supposed to be an art, and I have yet to see a course longer than 7,000 yards that calls for artful execution. Shot-making doesn't count for anything. You just see how far you can hit it off the tee at a wide-open fairway, and if you miss the fairway you've still got a shot because there isn't enough trouble to make you think twice. It's a great game for gorillas.

The greens on these monster courses today are big enough to build a guest house on. Don't invite me to be your guest, though. They eliminate chipping and make putting more than half the game. They're built by machines, so they don't have any subtle rolls and breaks in them. You can hit a driver for your second shot and have a great chance to put it some-where on the green. You might be 200 feet from the hole but you're on the green, baby. That isn't golf. It also isn't good economics to have to maintain 16,000-foot greens in a day when the cost of help is driving one private club after another out of business and discouraging many cities from building needed courses.

It doesn't have to be that hard to build a course that can play equally well for tour players and members. Long tees give you flexibility. They don't have to be as long as those of Trent Jones. We want a 6,500-yard course that will stretch to 6,900 for the pros. Strangely, when designers stretch an existing course, they tend to take a strong hole that's already a good match for the pros and stretch it, instead of taking one of the cripples and beefing it up. Don't ask me why. They'll take a par-4 hole that already plays 420 and make it 450. What they ought to do is take a hole that plays 360, forget about distance, and turn it into a tight driving hole. String four or five fairway bunkers out there where the pro can reach them if he tries to

113

let out the shaft and shortcut his drive. Or throw in a small lake at a strategic spot. Put this trouble where the member won't be reaching it. It may not be quite as easy and cheap, but it's going to improve the golf course for everybody.

Put more thought into the greens and the trouble around them. Build smaller greens that offer more options. On that 360-yard hole we just talked about, the pro will be going at the green with a short iron and the member with a middle iron. That's fine. Set deep bunkers up into the sides of the green, with the green sloping off toward the sand, and allow for pin positions close to the sand for the pros. Leave an opening in the front of the green so the average player can run the ball on. You can put a pin position in the middle of the green for him, away from the trouble.

Over all, a golf course has to have good pace and flow. You don't want three straight 420-yard par-4s. Variety is the spice of a course, especially in the par-4s because there will probably be ten of them. To start with, a par-4 should be demanding off the tee. I like the idea of having an equal number of par-4s doglegging to the right and to the left. That way the course won't favor the player who draws everything from right to left or fades everything from left to right.

The hazards—bunkers or water or alligators or what-ever—should be far enough off the tee and far enough apart so you can use your driver. The Rio Pinar course where we play in Orlando has a 450-yard par-4 that leaves you about twenty yards of driving area between bunkers, right where you'd expect to land a good drive. What in hell kind of argument does a man have to have with his wife to go and lay out a hole like that? Why didn't he just fill the fairway with water for 250 yards and then nobody could have driven the ball. The way it is you have to lay up off the tee and then hit a long iron or wood into the green. For my money, nobody should ever have to hit a wood into a green if he's hit a decent drive. The green has one bunker and it's thirty yards short, so any pro

114

can scald any kind of a shot and hit the green, but the upshot is that the hole first penalizes a good drive and then rewards a mediocre second shot, and that's a poor excuse for architecture.

I like to see a hundred-yard swing in the length of the par-4s on a course, from 360 yards to 460. Your short par-4s should be designed much differently from your long ones, though they often aren't. The short par-4s should have tight driving areas. Put fairway bunkers where they will keep a man honest, and make them fairly deep without being completely penal. Leave the man a chance to get onto the green but make him hit a difficult shot. The greens on short par-4s should be small and well-bunkered. A green with two or three different levels is good for these holes. A good player shouldn't be able to miss a short-iron shot by more than ten yards in any direction and not be in jail, in a bunker or in the water or down a bank in tall grass. A pushed or pulled shot should go into a bunker. A shot that's short or long should be on the wrong level of the green, giving him a testy putt.

On some of your best par-4s a golfer might be hitting only a wedge to the green. The seventh hole at Augusta National is a prime example. It's a 3-wood and a wedge. But you'd better hit two damn good shots or you can make 6 faster than you can count the strokes. The drive has to be positioned to leave you a shot that's clear of overhanging trees alongside the narrow fairway. The green is tiny and elevated and sharply tiered. It's guarded by deep bunkers almost all the way around. If you catch your iron shot a trifle fat, you're in one of those bunkers and the lip's taller than you are. I saw Charlie Coody get in a bunker on the seventh hole one year and take three shots to get out. He made seven and felt fortunate. I like the short par-4s at Augusta and also at Whitemarsh and Atlanta Country Club. They're often followed by long par-4s, which is good pacing.

The long par-4s should give you more leeway in the driving

area. The fairway bunkers should be shallower, because you're going to have to be coming with a long iron to get close to the green. You should have a chance to reach the green with an excellent shot, because the player who drives it more off line and misses the bunker will probably have that chance. The architects tend to put the tough bunkers on the long par-4s and the easy bunkers on the short par-4s. If I weren't so dumb, I'd think they have it backwards. On a lot of new courses none of the bunkers is deep. It's cheaper to maintain bunkers with a machine than by hand, and you can't get into those deep old bunkers with a machine.

The green should be bigger on a long par-4, because you shouldn't be penalized as severely for missing a long-iron shot as a short-iron shot, and you ought to have to use every club in your bag on a good course.

You can't stop a long-iron shot on a small green; you can't get enough backspin and height on the ball. The tenth hole at Oakland Hills near Detroit, the site of the 1972 PGA Championship, is a great long par-4. It's tough but fair, 459 yards. The tee is elevated about twenty feet. Your drive has to carry traps that edge into the fairway on the right side in order to finish in the best position for your second shot. You can be hitting as much as a 2-iron into the slightly elevated green, which is masterfully bunkered on both sides. You earn a par here, but if you get bogey you don't feel it was anybody's fault but your own.

Augusta, for all its outstanding holes, has two of the most unfair long par-4s I know. The tenth hole demands a long hook off the tee, and you still will probably wind up with a downhill lie for a long second shot to an elevated green. Hook the ball too much and you're in the tall trees. The green is always so hard that the ball rarely holds. It's the toughest green on the course to 2-putt from 35 feet because it's in the shade and poorly maintained. Some years it has almost no grass. The fifth hole is another bad long par-4. It's a driver

116

and a 2-iron for anybody whose name isn't Jack Nicklaus or Godzilla, and the green rises and then slopes away. If you carry the ball onto the green, it inevitably will run into the bunker at the back left or run off the green to the right. The only way for most players to play the hole is to land the ball twenty yards short of the green, dead on line with the center of the green, and run it on. The hole is a bad test.

I don't think you ever should have to hit a wood on a par-3 hole, whether you're a pro or a weekender. A par-3 should be an iron shot, a tactical challenge rather than a muscle contest. It should never be longer than 180 yards.

I'm not suggesting that par-3s be easy letup holes. You should have to think and execute with precision to get your par. The green ought to be small, never bigger than 5,000 feet. It should be protected as fully as a high school girl's virginity, with bunkers or water or both. Elevate the green to complicate the player's judging of distance and club selection. Build two levels into the green and give it subtle contouring. A player hitting a short iron to a green should have to do something extra with the shot. If he misses the hole by twenty feet, he should have a tricky putt, not a high-percentage birdie putt. Make him putt through a hollow or something.

If you insist on having par-3s that are 200 yards and longer, give the player a bigger target. Most players will have to hit a 3-wood on a nice day and a driver if the wind is blowing against them, and you don't pinpoint shots like that. Make the green large and flat and minimize the trouble, especially in front. Ordinarily you should have to carry the ball onto the green on the fly on a par-3, but if you're hitting a big wood you need that margin of error. Elevating the tee can give the player a better view of the hole and cause it to play shorter than that asinine length it's listed at.

An example of a par-3 that's too long is the fourth hole at Whitemarsh, where the Philadelphia tournament is played. It's a true 235 yards, the wind is often against you, there's water all down the right side, you have a tough bunker on the left and out-of-bounds just behind the green, and the green is small with a deep swale undulating through its center. The green can dry out and make it nearly impossible to hit without bouncing over and going out of bounds. Bobby Nichols suffered what may well have been the most embarrassing time of his career on this hole in 1965. He made an 8—and never went in the water! He hit his first two shots over the green and out of bounds.

If you can play the fourth hole at Whitemarsh in twelve strokes for four rounds, you really have achieved something. The only man I ever saw play the hole perfectly was Ben Hogan back in the late 1950s, and he hit a driver in there every day. If the hole were played at 180 yards so you could carry an iron onto the green, it would be a tremendous test. But as it is, it's closer to being a par-4 than a par-3. I refuse to hit a wood on the hole, no matter how hard the wind is blowing into me. I lay up. I take a 1-iron knowing I can't knock the ball through the green and out of bounds. I aim at the left-hand bunker, away from the water on the right, and try to put it in the bunker or just short of it. If I get my fade, I'll be on the green, but I don't count on it.

Having roasted Whitemarsh for its unwieldy fourth hole, I would like to say that Whitemarsh has the best group of par-3 holes on the tour. Besides the fourth hole, which I prefer to forget, they measure 125, 145, and 175 yards, a nice variety of par-3 length. You might play a wedge to the ninth hole because it plays 15 to 25 yards shorter than the 125 yards it's supposed to be. But the hole demands finesse. The pistol-shaped green is small and surrounded by six bunkers. The green slopes off toward the bunkers. It's a definite birdie hole—but only if you can bring off a classy touch shot. The twelfth hole is 175 yards and the toughest on the course. There's out-of-bounds on the right and a steep hill on the left, and you often get a crosswind. The green is long and narrow

118

and hard to hit, but it slopes in from both sides, and if you do hit it you'll end up close to the hole. Tom Weiskopf beat me by one stroke in the 1971 Philadelphia Golf Classic by playing the 145-yard sixteenth hole 3 under par, but I still like the hole (I'm not sure if I still like Tom). It's a deceptive hole because the green is about 100 feet higher than the tee. Often the pin position is on the right, which brings into play a large tree in front of the green. There are traps on both sides. The green slopes sharply from back to front and putts from above the hole are hard to contain. These three par-3s at Whitemarsh almost never require more than a middle iron from a pro or an average golfer.

Can a par-3 be too short? Sure. I think 120 yards is a good cutoff point unless there are extenuating circumstances. Atlanta has a mini-par-3 of 120 yards that drops off at least a hundred feet from tee to green and plays at a half sand wedge sometimes, but the target is so small and the distance so tricky to judge because of the elevation of the tee that it's a fun challenge.

A good par-5 should give a man a challenge and also a choice. I'm speaking now of the second shot. You should have the option—the existential predicament, whatever you want to call it—to go for the green or lay up. Most par-5s are designed either so it's easy to reach the green with two long shots or so you are forced to play short of the green in two. I like to have the choice to gamble or not to gamble. I expect to pay a high price if I gamble and fail. I should have to hit a very good second shot to reach the green. If I hit anything less, I should be penalized at least a stroke by going in the water or out of bounds.

Basically, a good par-5 is designed for three shots and two putts. The green should be small to challenge a short third shot or a long, gambling second shot. In either case, a man should have to hit a good shot.

But it's that choice with the second shot that intrigues me.

Tucson National is an example of a course that is less exciting than it could be because you get no options on the par-5s. There are bunkers way short of the green and again up close to the green, with not enough room in between. You either have to lay up way short with your second shot or have to overextend yourself trying to reach a green that is too far away.

All the par-5s at Augusta National are outstanding, but the fifteenth is truly great. It never restricts you—it lets you do as much as your ability and guts can bite off. If you hit a super drive and second shot, you'll be putting for an eagle. If you don't, God love you. Your ball will be in the water or worse. A fine shot is rewarded and a poor one is penalized, and that's what course architecture ought to be all about. The crowds love it; thousands fill the grandstand at the fifteenth during the Masters and line both sides of the fairway at 8 o'clock in the morning and never move all day except to get a sandwich or use the bathroom. They can tell you every detail of Gene Sarazen's famous double eagle on the fifteenth in 1935 —you'd think every one of them saw it.

The hole is 520 yards maximum, but the green is fronted by a big pond and slopes off quickly on all sides. You're hitting a long iron or a wood second if you go for it. If you go over the green, your ball can run all the way into the pond on the sixteenth hole. The green is crowned in the center, making it all the more difficult to hold. Usually on the last day the pin will be tucked in the narrow deck on the front left of the green. If you're short of the hole, your ball can roll back into the pond. If you're past the hole, you have to chip or putt down a swift hill toward that same water. It isn't an easy par-5 even if you lay up, because you have trouble finding a flat lie to pitch from. It's the single most dramatic hole in golf to me.

We need more great holes, more great courses on the tour. We play really undistinguished courses in tournaments like Phoenix, Houston, the Bob Hope, Orlando, and Hartford.

120

We should be playing on all fine courses. It's good for the players and good for the fans who can see the courses on television. There are many reasons why we aren't doing so. Great courses often belong to very private clubs, and the members value their privacy more than they value the hoopla of a tour event. Joe Dey made a strong effort as tour commissioner to improve the quality of the courses. Getting the old Los Angeles Open moved from a mediocre Rancho Park municipal track to prestigious Riviera was a tremendous trade. It was almost tremendous enough to make me excuse the role Joe played, when he was at the USGA, in giving the U.S. Open to Hazeltine.

NICKLAUS

I would like to see Jack Nicklaus win the Grand Slam—the four major tournaments in the same year—for the simple reason that he is capable of doing it. It's his one remaining goal and I hope he fulfills it. I ought to hope he fulfills it soon. Maybe then he would feel he had no more worlds to capture and would retire and leave the tour to us mortals.

Nicklaus is playing a different game than the rest of us. Any year he doesn't win two major tournaments has to be a bad year for him in his own mind. Jack would rather win one major title than five lesser ones. He knows he'll be remembered by the number of major championships he wins. Sam Snead has won 28 more championships than Ben Hogan, but Hogan always ranks ahead of Snead when you're debating greatness because Hogan won all the big ones.

As good as Hogan was, I don't think he or anyone else is close to Nicklaus as an all-time great. Nicklaus has much more physical equipment than Hogan had and he's maturing into just as good a strategist. Jack hits the ball so well that people don't appreciate that he thinks his way around a golf course better than anybody else on the tour today.

Jack's still a young man, in his 30s. Hogan was only beginning to do his thing well at that stage of life. Nicklaus is pacing himself, playing only 20 to 25 tournaments a year, and I expect him to be beating everybody in fifteen years. He could be another Sam Snead if his desire holds up. He's building a unique business empire and he has to keep winning to make it go. That's a keen incentive.

When Jack is playing well, nobody beats him. Not Tom Weiskopf or Johnny Miller or me or anybody else. He knows it and we know it. We don't talk about it in those terms, but we accept it as a fact of life. I'm not saying the rest of us have written ourselves off against Jack. He's human, and if he's a little off and I play up to my capacity and make all my putts, I can beat him. But he has to be almost mediocre to lose.

He's the only man on tour who can make two or three straight bogeys and then turn his round right around with two or three quick birdies. It all starts with his tremendous tee ball. He has more accurate length than anyone else. We have several players who can move the ball 300 yards off the tee. Jim Dent can hit it 350 with a three-quarter swing. Larry Ziegler, Bobby Nichols, Eddie Pearce—all of them can hit it a ton. The difference is that Nicklaus can hit it far and consistently straight and carry the ball higher. He's having some lower-back problems that seem to be costing him a little power but not that much.

He beats you to death on the par-5s. They're damn near eagle holes for him. On most courses he can count on birdieing at least three of the four par-5s, and he's going to make some eagles hitting the green in 2. On a lot of par-5s he can hit a driver and a middle iron. On a long course like Firestone

—which is generally considered a great test but is too dull by my standards—he has to be a huge favorite. On the second hole, for instance, a par-5 that doglegs left, I'll hit a driver and 3-wood and be short of the green. He can cream his driver over the trees at the corner of the dogleg and have an iron to the green. If we were in a playoff, I'd feel like walking straight into the clubhouse.

Nicklaus has an advantage on longer par-3s because he hits his long irons so high that he can drop them softly on the green when I'm hitting a 3-wood that will hit and run. A high ball isn't good—except when Nicklaus hits it. He can hit the ball high and still hold it on line in the wind. The ball doesn't sail or hang up on him.

On par-4s he has an edge because he can carry the fairway trouble with his high driver shots. The bunkers and water hazards are out there 250 to 260 yards, where most pros drive the ball. Nicklaus flies the ball over all that trouble. He flat air-mails it. Recently we played a course that is typical. The par-4s were bunkered left and right and everybody was playing in between the bunkers. Nicklaus simply flew the fairway bunker that was on the shortest route to the green.

The only way to equalize these conditions between Nicklaus and me would be to stagger a series of fairway bunkers from 250 on out to 280 yards and taper them into the fairway so that he would have to contend with the same number of hazards as everyone else. Make the first two bunkers shallow and the last two deeper. Or if you're talking about a lateral water hazard, extend it farther toward the green and cut it out into the fairway more so that the farther you hit the drive the greater the risk you run. None of this would affect the playability of the course for the average golfer—he'll be driving the ball short of the trouble. Then Nicklaus would have to work for his distance the same as everyone else.

Another thing about Jack's driving. He can afford to let out because he's stronger out of the rough. Long grass doesn't bother him the way it does us shorter players. He can go for the green where another player can't do anything but chop the ball back to the fairway. That's why he's particularly tough in the U.S. Open. The U.S. Golf Association grows dense rough everywhere you look; but you don't see Nicklaus losing many strokes in the rough.

Nicklaus' power swing is the modern action. It's right for him, but I think thousands of average players are making a mistake trying to emulate Jack's swing, especially his overly upright plane. He forces the club up and out of a natural 45-degree plane on his backswing, letting his right elbow fly out away from his body. For the average player that's disaster. For Jack it works to give him a bigger swing arc because he is able to make well-timed adjustments at the start of his downswing.

Jack is a body player. He uses the big muscles. He's a hitter, not a swinger. He creates tremendous torque on his backswing by turning well with his upper body but resisting with his legs. Then on the downswing he uses his legs mightily. He is the ultimate legs player. His unusual physique has all but dictated that he build a swing on strong leg action. His secret, physically, is that he's four inches short of normal in the thighs and upper arms for a man of his girth. He's 5 feet 11 inches and 185 pounds. His thighs are massive; they're 29 inches around, which just happens to be my waist size. He has me in the thighs by a foot! The man is abnormally built, and that has a lot to do with his power.

He has his swing so well grooved that he gives the appearance of being almost mechanical. His movements appear to be programmed. He may not be the most elegant looking swinger on the tour, but he stays in good balance through the ball and there is a great freedom of motion in his swing.

His finesse is underrated. His putting touch on fast greens is unbelievable. He rolls it so well from 20 feet. I'm better on slow greens because I don't have a nice fluid stroke. When I can rap the ball, I can get it on line. My stroke isn't a smooth, repeating stroke, and on slow greens you can get away with making a little different hit every time. On fast greens you can't, and on fast greens he is the best. And he's the best lag putter, getting long putts from 30 to 100 feet to within "gimme" distance of the hole. He wouldn't 3-putt a super-market parking lot.

I wouldn't rate Jack the best putter in the world overall because he doesn't put that much pressure on his putting. He hits so many greens in regulation figures that he doesn't have to sink a lot of putts to beat you. I will say that if I had to have somebody putt a twenty-footer for everything I own—my house, my cars, my family—I'd want Nicklaus to putt it for me.

Jack can't tell you why he makes so many crucial putts, except he works harder on them mentally. It's painful watching his concentration. He can stand over a putt for 40 seconds before he pulls the trigger. If I did that, I'd freeze. It would drive me up the wall. But he isn't aware of the time passing.

A friend of Jack's told me something that points up his unusual power of concentration. Few people realize that Jack smokes two packs of cigarettes a day. He's almost a chain smoker. But he doesn't smoke while he's playing—maybe because he's afraid he'll be a bad influence on young people—and he concentrates so hard on his golf that he doesn't miss smoking!

Does Nicklaus have a weakness? He has a glaring weakness. From 100 yards in to the green he is one of the poorer wedge players on the tour. He is very weak pitching the ball with a three-quarter swing. A player like Lee Trevino is much better at these shorter finesse shots than Jack.

The three-quarter shot is a feel shot. Jack has no feel in his pitch shots and sand shots. It certainly is something he could learn—but his idea of how to play a pitch shot is wrong in my opinion. His full swings are correctly based on leg action. Whenever he's playing bad golf he thinks it's because his legs aren't moving enough on the downswing. They start forward before his hands finish going back.

He tries to play short shots the same way, and you can't. You don't play those little shots with your legs, you play them with your hands. Your legs do move some, but you don't drive them hard toward the target. Jack tries to feel a 30-yard pitch shot through his legs when he should feel it through his hands. He treats a pitch shot too much like a power shot and that's why he isn't a good wedge player. It's why he doesn't win as much on shorter courses.

How is Jack as a playing partner? One of the best. He is exceptionally courteous and friendly; he always has been, despite his public image as a somewhat aloof, cold person. He always thinks to compliment you on a good shot, and has something pleasant to say when there's a wait on the tee. His galleries aren't as boisterous as Arnold Palmer's always have been, but they get bigger every year with more people coming to appreciate his ability, and he goes out of his way to see that they don't bother you. Often he will let you putt out first even though it's his turn. That keeps the gallery from running to the next tee.

As well as Jack has played recently, I don't think he's struck the ball as well the past six years as he did the six years before. But he's learned to accept it and he uses his head much better. As a strategist I can't imagine anyone but Hogan ever comparing with Jack. He almost never stops thinking during a round. He's always driving the ball at a small target, not just down the center. He doesn't let a bad shot bother him—as soon as he believes he understands what he did wrong, he turns his entire attention to the next shot. He can maneuver the ball. He likes to play a fade for control, but can draw the ball from right to left if he wants to. At Augusta he draws his drives because it's a right-to-left course. Most players can play only one way or the other.

He's a great playing partner, but I hate to be paired with

him down the stretch in a tournament if we're both in contention because his power makes you feel so inadequate. You tend to start pressing to hit it as far as he does, and then you're off your game. He's a slow player but faster than many others. He walks very fast; he's slow over the ball. Other than that, he's a model partner.

It's funny about the superstars' personalities off the course. The fans assume that Arnold Palmer is great company and Nicklaus is a bore. Arnold has much more charisma on the course; he can look at you if you're in the gallery and you think you've been friends, or lovers, for life. Arnold has more expressions than a French mimic if he misses a shot, and the fans feel for him. Jack is changing, but he's essentially still the opposite of Arnold as a public personality: serious, all business.

But off the course, Jack is much more fun as a dinner companion than Arnold, or at least that's been my limited experience. I don't dine regularly with either Arnold or Jack, but I find Jack a stimulating man who can talk about many subjects. Arnold is fun but he seldom thinks about anything but golf. I understand he has only a dozen books in his house—and they're all golf books. Jack enjoys interesting people who aren't in golf. He's not funny, but he has a little dry wit. He's straightforward. If something's bugging him, he says so, but he doesn't hold grudges.

We had dinner at La Costa one night during the Tournament of Champions and it was one of the most pleasant evenings I have had. Both of us are amateur wine buffs and we drank and discussed good wine. Jack has started his own wine collection and I intend to start one. When the wine steward started to pour the wine without letting it set open for several minutes, we straightened him out. Jack talked about his changing business ventures and how the demands on him are growing. I think he thoroughly relishes his bright new image, and I don't blame him at all. He joined the tour as the big fat boy who had been raised with a silver 7-iron in his mouth, and one of the first things he did was upset Palmer, everybody's hero, in the 1962 U.S. Open at Oakmont. He didn't like to talk to the press and, since the press likes to be catered to, that cost him. I think he eventually would have won over the fans anyway—it's hard to dislike the best player in history—but he speeded the process a few years ago when he lost a lot of weight, let his hair grow, started dressing better, and developed into a good interview for the writers. All of a sudden Jack Nicklaus was sexy, of all things.

I think the big turning point in his career came when his father died early in 1970. Jack and his father were very close, and his father had lived for Jack's golf. When he died, Jack felt that he had let his father down. Jack says he sat down and reexamined his values and determined to be the greatest golfer ever.

The things Jack can do now under the most terrifying pressure are the real mark of his greatness. They keep coming back to me. I'll never forget the 1972 U.S. Open at Pebble Beach, the final day. The course was unfairly tricked up, and the seventeenth hole, a par-3 over 200 yards long into the roar of a frigid ocean gale, was the worst hole of all. The green offered little landing area and was circled by deep bunkers and grass so high you literally could lose a ball in it if you missed the green by three feet. I came off the course complaining to a friend that he ought to go out and look at the seventeenth hole if he wanted to see a perfect example of how the USGA can screw up paradise. I think I made 5 there and felt lucky.

Nicklaus later came to the seventeenth tee in a close fight for the championship. Many players were aiming at the bunker in front of the green rather than risk burying the ball in the tall grass. So Jack took a 1-iron—and hit the stick about three inches above the cup! The birdie gave him the tournament. I was watching on television and that's the damnedest pressure shot I've ever seen. He was probably kicking himself for not holing the shot on the fly. With his golden hair flying in the wind, he looked like a Nordic king.

He has found that his new image and record in the major tournaments are highly marketable commodities. During the first part of his career he was managed by Mark McCormack, the Cleveland lawyer who has Arnold Palmer and a vast assortment of other sports and entertainment celebrities. I don't know the full story behind Jack's leaving McCormack, but I always figured it would be difficult for McCormack to do justice by anybody but Palmer. Palmer was his first major client and they're close friends, and I imagine Jack understandably feels he was slighted. As for Mr. McCormack, I think anybody who would let Nicklaus get away should run straight for home and have his wife hit him over the head with a rolling pin. I'm sure Nicklaus made a lot of money for McCormack and probably vice versa. Jack obviously concluded that he could do better on his own, and I'm sure he is correct.

When a player reaches the stature of a Nicklaus, it's time for him to have his own personal manager and not be part of a stable. I think Jack should have jumped sooner, after he won his first Open. Jack has set up a fast-moving organization of his own that isn't quite like anything else in golf, and he's making money faster than the trucks can carry it to the bank. I've heard good guesses that he makes $3 million a year in non-golf income from endorsements and other enterprises around the world, everything from shoes to course building.

I don't know whether Nicklaus or Palmer is making more money off the golf course. I'm sure Jack is catching up fast if he isn't already ahead of Arnold.

Arnold is assured of being filthy rich the rest of his life no matter what happens. Jack doesn't talk much about it but I have no doubt his old, friendly rivalry with Palmer is as hot at the bank as it ever was on the course. Jack is dead set on proving he can do better at McCormack's business than McCormack can, and the early returns look good for Jack. He has assembled a team of bright, energetic specialists—one in publishing, one in banking, one in law, one in advertising, one in something else. These guys develop nothing but first-rate, long-term, top-dollar involvements with companies like Pontiac, Hart Schaffner & Marx, *Golf Digest,* and American Express.

What Jack doesn't know about business, these guys are supposed to. Nicklaus is quite shrewd about dealing with the people who work for him. For the most part, they get paid commissions for the deals they engineer, everything to be approved in total by Jack. Jack has nothing to lose.

Nicklaus seems to thrive on the diversion of big business. He likes to get completely away from golf with his family and business in Palm Beach and then return to the tour rejuvenated. I don't think his business interests will hurt his career unless they expand too rapidly for him to control.

His swelling business empire worries me in another way, though. I can see Jack getting into potential conflicts of interest with the tour if he isn't awfully careful. He is associated with John Montgomery who handles a dozen tour events, including Nicklaus' own tournament in Ohio. Jack's people are handling some other well-known players, such as Tom Weiskopf and Ben Crenshaw. Jack and his helpers are legally within their rights, I'm sure. They're too smart not to be.

Jack already dominates us with his talent, and his business empire gives him added incentive to keep playing well. In ten years he's liable to own the tour.

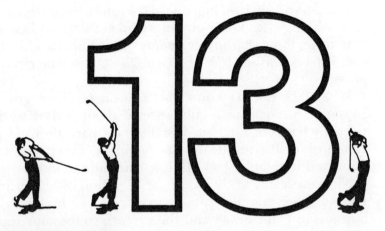

THE FIELD

Now I'll give you my impressions of some of the other players on the tour you have heard about. Some of them no doubt will want equal time. You can't live with people day after day without learning more about them than you ever wanted to know. Some of them might not like what I have to say, but that never did stop me, so here goes.

Tommy Aaron Too nice a guy for the tour. He doesn't have a strong enough winning instinct. He would never say or do anything to hurt anybody.

Tommy has been second more times than I can count, and it bothers him more than he lets on. Not even winning the Masters in 1973 could change his reputation as Tommy Runner-up. It's an unfair tag. He was stuck with the brides-maid image early in his career when he lost a couple of dramatic playoffs to Tony Lema and Arnold Palmer. He points out that Jack Nicklaus has finished second many more times than he has and that second is a lot better than third. He's right, of course, but the public isn't listening.

His full swing is long and rhythmic, and Sam Snead has picked it as the best on the tour. It's much like Sam's in its smoothness. Tommy is fundamentally sound but sometimes loses the club at the top and can't coordinate his downswing. When that happens he hits a lot of high pull-hooks. In the last two years he has shortened his swing some and firmed up his action.

Tommy has an apt expression for hitting too much from the top of the swing and dissipating his power before impact. He says he "ejaculated prematurely."

Buddy Allin A sincere young player who was on the Brigham Young University team with Johnny Miller, then went into the Army and served in Vietnam as an artillery officer. He was decorated six times and I understand was in some terrible action. Buddy won't talk about Vietnam, which makes me believe it.

He gets good distance for a 130-pounder. Uses his shoulders very emphatically.

George Archer George has got more out of his game over the years than anybody else on the tour. Because he's six feet six inches tall, it's tough for him to stay in balance. He's too ungainly for a golfer, and I wouldn't trade swings with him for $100,000. He makes absolutely no hip turn.

But George has the finest short game I have seen. He can scramble all day. He trusts what he has going for him and isn't bothered when he makes a bad drive or approach shot. From fifteen feet, he's death, and that's where you score. He's very still over the ball and strokes with only his arms and shoulders.

I'm afraid George puts so much pressure on his long game that his nerves are going to desert him on his short game before too long.

His personal life will never hurt his nerves. George's idea of a big night out is a hamburger at McDonald's and a science fiction movie. He leads the tour in attending movies and has an elaborate rating system worked out. George does have one vice. When he has trouble sleeping during a tournament, he smokes one cigarette. "It makes me so dizzy I doze right off," he says.

George has a laconic sense of humor that makes him fun to be around. One day he started a round horribly but finished strong for a score in the low 60s. One of the other players asked him what the turning point had been. "When I popped a couple of Rolaids," George said.

Miller Barber He's "Mr. X." Before he married in his late 30s, Miller would quietly disappear at night with mysterious female company and nobody could ever find him for dinner or a card game.

His swing is one of the two worst actions on the tour. I don't see how he keeps from breaking his left arm on his backswing, closing the face of the club and looping it to the top. Then he loops it back down. But Miller's swing works because he is consistent—he repeats it every time.

Frank Beard He is one of the few truly bright men playing the tour. After a few scotches his quick, cynical sense of humor can zing you good. I enjoy bridge games with him.

Beard's game is simple. He aims fifteen yards right of his target and hooks the ball back in where he wants it. He likes to tell a story about Bobby Locke, the old South African who used to hook everything, including his putts. Locke once started a drive to the right, over an out-of-bounds. The crowd gasped but Locke calmly said, "Don't worry, that SOB will be back." And it hooked back.

Beard's grip is bad. It's a hooker's grip, a strong left-hand grip (turned to the right on the club). He got away with it for years because he had great tempo. The one bad slump Beard has had came late in his career when he tried to stop hitting the sweeping hook and start hitting his shots straight.

Philosophically, Frank and I are about eight million miles apart. He is forever saying golf is a business, he doesn't want to be bothered by the public, and the game is no fun. He takes himself and the game too seriously.

I get sick of all his talk about money, money, money. I doubt that he can remember the last time he picked up a check. He has the deepest pockets and the shortest arms anywhere.

Gay Brewer A good ole boy liked by everybody. He rivals Miller Barber for having the worst swing on the tour that gets results. He swings the club in a figure eight. If you didn't know better you'd swear he was trying to kill snakes. But his swing is grooved.

Gay plays better outside the country. He has won a small fortune in fall tournaments in Britain and Japan.

Bill Casper Unfortunately a falling star. For years I considered Casper the most underrated player on the tour. When Palmer and Player and Nicklaus were getting headlines as the Big Three, a label trumped up by their business manager with little justification, Casper was playing better golf. Check the stroke averages, the best measure. He never got the ink because he didn't have Mark McCormack managing him and he didn't have as much personality as a glass of water. Then Casper decided golf wasn't as important to him as other activities, including his family, his adopted religion, fishing, chasing back and forth to give golf lessons to the King of Morocco, and who knows what else. He stopped winning, got fat, and quickly went from being barely noticed to being unnoticed.

Casper is an odd guy. I like him on some counts and don't like him on some others. Everybody thinks he is an easygoing, dull sort of person, but that isn't so.

Billy grew up as something of a young roustabout in San

Diego; inside of that distinguished looking large man with the grey sideburns is a hell-raiser trying to get out.

Billy may think religion has helped his golf, but you have to be confused in the first place to think that religion will help you hit a better golf shot. That's like a Catholic fighter crossing himself coming into the ring. It's great if he can fight.

Some players simply cannot admit to themselves that they can make a bad shot. They have to blame it on somebody or something else. Casper is the worst that way. In his own mind I doubt that he has ever hit a bad golf shot that was his fault. He's a front-runner. The front-runner sets up alibis even before he needs them. Then if he wins he is doubly heroic. If he loses he has a ready-made excuse. Lee Trevino is also somewhat of a front-runner. I've been a front-runner myself. It's frightening to think about winning against the best golfers in the world. It takes great courage to get in position to win and then go ahead and do it without choking. But it's one thing to make excuses to yourself and another thing to make them to the public, which ought to get smart about these guys.

Casper has been a great putter but he always says he's a poor one. That grates on a lot of the rest of us out here. Personally I would love to be known as a great putter. Unfortunately, I'm like a teddy bear with boxing gloves on the green. Billy does have a strange putting stroke. He picks the putter almost straight up instead of keeping it low as most great putters do. He raps down on the ball instead of stroking through it. But the key is that he putts the same way every time. He has amazing consistency and touch. His putting nerves show no indication of letting him down. He's a great putter and the next time I hear him say he is a lousy putter I may throw a ball at him.

His big swing also is unusual. He starts with a Harley-Davidson grip, his left hand turned way over to the right like a motorcycle rider. He plays from shut to open with the club-face, scissoring into the ball. He lets the left hand break upward just after impact to keep from hooking, but lately he has been hitting a lot of hooks anyway. On his downswing his hip action is distinctive. I could tell Billy's downswing from an airplane at 30,000 feet. He just slides his left hip instead of turning it and sort of bumps onto his left side. Billy usually can get away with these idiosyncracies because he has a pattycake swing—to use his own description—and his action is, like his putting stroke, very repetitive.

If he rededicates himself to golf, I think Billy can last a lot longer than Palmer and even Trevino.

Jim Colbert An optimistic little guy who is always trying to sell you something. Since I have known him, he has fronted for a newfangled "potato masher" putter, a charter plane operation to take pros and their families from one tournament to the next, copper bracelets, a new golf magazine, land speculation, and I forget what all else. Usually Jim goes into these deals with his good buddy Dean Refram, another energetic little man, who was a pretty fair player until croquet-style putting was outlawed.

Jim is wildly inconsistent. He often plays well in important tournaments like the U.S. Open.

Charles Coody Closer with a dollar than anybody else on tour except his pal Frank Beard. Charles is a pleasant fellow, though.

Beard kiddingly calls him a little old lady. Charles goes to bed precisely twelve hours before he is going to tee off. He keeps careful accounts of all the money he spends; he once spent an entire evening looking for a penny he had lost in his accounting. He finally learned his wife had spent it for bubble gum. When Coody won the Masters, Beard said, "That $25,-000 is out of circulation."

Charles also is highly superstitious. He wears lucky slacks, marks his ball with a lucky coin, eats the same breakfast every morning as long as he's playing well, and tugs at his clothes about three dozen times in a certain routine before he finally hits each shot. He keeps records on every round he plays —how many fairways and greens he hit, how many times he was in sand, penalty strokes, and so on.

Bruce Crampton A player who puts out no phony baloney and who has the worst image on the tour. He's one of the few people I know who you can look at for the first time and dislike. He's cold and deliberate and he can be rude to little people when he isn't getting his way. He's an only child and a spoiled man. He can be so bad to a marshall or a press photographer that he embarrasses me, and I'm hard to embarrass.

But I like Bruce. He's the most misunderstood guy on the tour. His redeeming virtues are his total honesty and his tremendous consistency as a golfer.

Bruce is the son of an Australian policeman and was raised to live by the rules whatever he is doing. Bruce probably knows the rules better than anybody else out here, and he's every bit as tough on himself as he is on anybody else. He lost a tournament in Indiana one year because he called an obscure penalty on himself that would otherwise have gone unnoticed.

Bruce's problem is lack of style. He doesn't know how to communicate with people without seeming to be abrasive. His natural expression is kind of a half sneer: his jaw and teeth are set in such a way that they make him look meaner than he is. He's so serious about his game that he has trouble seeing the humor in life in general. He was a sickly child and I'm sure that influenced his dour personality.

If he tries, Bruce can be gracious and kind. He can be so nice sometimes I don't believe it. He's a real Dr. Jekyll and Mr. Hyde.

His swing tempo is the best on the tour. His tempo never varies from the first hole of a tournament to the 72nd, from a driver to a wedge. I've never seen him lose that great consistent rhythm. He coordinates the upper and lower halves of his body more smoothly than anybody else. Bruce is a very strong, well-conditioned athlete, built like a football running back with powerful shoulder and chest development. He's an upper-body player, the opposite of Nicklaus. He always swings well within himself, using only 80 percent of his strength. That's a key to his superior tempo.

The mechanics of his swing are dead sound except for one factor. His hands are a little behind the ball at address, and the clubhead passes his hands coming into the ball. Therefore he's a little wristy and it isn't easy for him to hit a big fade when he wants to. He has trouble cutting his short-iron shots.

Bruce's putting can border on the incredible. He makes more twelve-foot putts for pars than any other three guys out here. He has to be the most underrated putter on the tour.

Ben Crenshaw Ben came out on the tour ready to win after several years of tough college and amateur competition and occasional pro tournaments. He cost himself a small fortune by staying in school as long as he did.

Crenshaw is a solid swinger and hits the ball long. His tempo is relaxed and will age well. He has a big, fluid swing, and he keeps the club on the ball a long time. He overswings when he's playing badly—takes the club back too far and loses a little control. In 1976 he was probably the best putter on the tour.

Ben is a nice, modest young man. The girls really go for his blond good looks, and it's a good thing for his career that he got married.

Jim Dent This big guy just knocks the dog water out of the ball. He's the longest hitter on the tour. Jack Nicklaus says Dent makes him feel inadequate. There is considerable loose talk about how far the pros can hit the ball; most of it is far-fetched. A stout drive for most of us is 260 yards under normal conditions. Nicklaus and a few others can pump it out there 300 when they want to. With the right conditions, Dent can hit it almost 400 yards. That's four football fields, fans.

Jim is a husky black, and as far as I'm concerned he's living, swinging proof that size *does* help you hit a golf ball for distance. No matter how good my timing is and how fast I swing, I'm not going to move the ball 400 yards. Unfortunately Jim is kind of like the 400-pound gorilla in that old golf joke. A big bet was made on the first tee on this gorilla. The gorilla drove the green on a 400-yard hole. Then he lined up his putt—and hit it 400 yards. Jim's short-iron game is something like that.

Bruce Devlin My favorite foreign player, Bruce is an Australian who lives in Florida now. He's friendly at all times, regardless of how he plays. He has the best temperament of all the pros, even though he has been a lousy physical specimen all his life. He had major surgery for varicose veins and has trouble walking a hilly course. If he gets caught in a 36-hole day because of a rainout, he barely makes it around. Because of his legs, he seldom practices. But he never complains.

Bruce says he gets his toughness from his father, a plumber in Australia (Bruce earned his master plumber's rating and worked for his father before turning pro). He tells great stories about hiding under bar stools while his father whipped rowdies, cops, and anybody else looking for a fight. His father once lost an arm, signed himself into the hospital, and was back at work in eleven days.

Bruce drives the ball well. His weakness is his short-iron game. He can put the ball as close to the hole with a 5-iron as with a 9-iron.

Bruce plays the tour only about half time nowadays, devoting the other half to course designing. He isn't like most other pros who lend their names to course architecture outfits. He's a working partner. You go into his office and his pockets are stuffed with blueprints.

140

Lee Elder Lee didn't have it nearly as tough as Charlie Sifford as a black man coming up in a white man's game, but he had it tough enough. He played the predominantly black United Golfers' Association tour and hustled for ten years before he saved enough of his own money to try the PGA tour at the age of 34.

I didn't care for the "controversies" he raised trying to get into the Masters, and I don't think he is appreciative enough of what Charlie Sifford has done for him and the other young blacks on the tour, but I like Lee. He's a cheerful, easygoing guy. He could sleep through the most important appointment of his life.

He's a short knocker but very straight off the tee. He has a strange double-overlap grip, two fingers of his right hand over the index finger of his left hand, to counter a hook. Also to protect against a hook he extends the clubhead out toward the target after impact longer than anybody else, so that his right hand never turns over his left. The result is a kind of rebound finish.

Ray Floyd Most people assume that Ray has partied his way out of a great career. He was twenty when he won the 1963 St. Petersburg Open in his rookie year, the youngest tour winner ever. He won the PGA Championship in 1969 and the Masters in a big way in 1976. I didn't think anybody would ever tie Nicklaus' Masters record—unless Nicklaus did.

There is no doubt Raymond can play the pants off everybody when he's hot. He can hit it long and he can hit it with finesse. The only explanation for his failure to become a superstar is that golf simply did not mean that much to him. He enjoys life and isn't as one-dimensional as the top players. He didn't work that hard at golf, and nobody plays this game well without working hard at it. But now he's married and has a family, and he's more stable. He says he wants to win. He can do it if he means it.

Ray has the kind of swing that needs plenty of tournament play. His tempo is fast, and if he doesn't watch it he doesn't give his feet and legs time to work.

Rod Funseth Color him grey. A nice guy, short on self-confidence. You know he can play because he can shoot some of the lowest numbers out here. But he plays cautiously and seems to be willing to settle for a good living. If Funseth shoots a 65 he will be thinking about how he might shoot 75 tomorrow.

Al Geiberger A shy person who has had plenty of problems, physically and domestically, but he hung in there and made a terrific comeback. Al is spindly and could stand to eat more peanut butter.

Bob Goalby The man I most like to be paired with. He extends courtesies to his playing partners that I have never seen elsewhere.

Here's an example you probably wouldn't notice watching a tournament on television. If I have a twelve-foot putt from the right side of the cup and he putts first from the other direction and runs his ball up a foot from the cup, he won't putt out; he'll mark his ball. Why? Because if I were to hit my twelve-footer past the hole I might have to putt back through the footprints he would leave making his tap-in.

David Graham I love to sit around and talk golf equipment and swing theory with David. He's an opinionated little devil.

David is from Australia and has traveled almost the entire world to play golf, and sometimes he acts as if he owns it. He'll be in a South American country where he can't speak the language and engage the entire hotel staff in a running battle over whether his breakfast eggs were cooked two minutes or two and a half minutes.

He doesn't know how good he has it. He comes to America

to make sacks of money on our tour. Then he goes to parties at tournaments and tells everyone how Americans aren't complete golfers because they don't play outside their homeland enough. That's known as bad-mouthing the hand that feeds you.

David is intense and is prone to nervous facial twitches. He tries to worry the game to conquer it, and sometimes he succeeds. He is going to be one of the game's most knowledgeable technicians. He tinkers with his clubs more than anybody except me and Arnold Palmer.

One of the few people David listens to is Bruce Devlin. Bruce has been a moderating influence on David and has smoothed some of the rough edges. Bruce got him a good deal representing a Florida resort. If David continues to follow Bruce's advice, he'll spare himself a lot of aggravation.

Lou Graham A friendly Tennesseean who can quietly sneak up on you and beat you. He has a controlled swing.

Hubert Green Another Southerner. He looks and acts Down Home but actually his family is from Birmingham high society. His dad was a doctor. He enjoys playing the part of a hillbilly but he's a hip hillbilly.

He's cocky and something of a smark-aleck. He likes to play too fast. Slow him down and he's less effective.

His game isn't much to look at. His swing is quick and too upright and he dips his shoulder coming down into the ball. Putting, he splits his hands on the shaft, spreads his legs, and hunkers over the ball like a chicken laying an egg.

Hubert is making good money right now—he won three in a row in early 1976—but he's like so many of these young pros who think they have the tour by the tail. Today he can play because his nerves are great. If he ever wakes up one morning and asks himself what the game's all about, he's in a bunch of trouble.

143

Hale Irwin He isn't large, wears horn-rimmed glasses, and looks like a bookworm, but Irwin was an All-Big Eight defensive football back at Colorado. He and Dick Anderson of the Miami Dolphins teamed in the secondary for the Buffs. Football helped prepare Irwin for golf because it made him a fiercer competitor. He fights you quietly on every stroke. He may be the best competitor on the tour, stroke for stroke.

Irwin has a decent golf swing. I don't like the way he cocks his wrists so late on his backswing and gets a lot of club flutter at the top. But he's very close to being on the same plane on his backswing and downswing, and that helps his consistency. He has a great release; he really can hit his fairway woods high. He plays well on tough courses and does not get flustered.

He has a tremendous short game and thinks his way around a course better than 99 percent of the players.

Don January He had to be the comeback of the year in 1976. Don is a slow-moving, slow-talking, slow-swinging Texan who left the tour for a couple of years to build golf courses, but when the economy went bad he came back. It's amazing that he was able to have a super year at the age of 46 after that long a layoff.

It helps that he has a long, smooth swing. Older fellows with short swings can lose too much distance.

Grier Jones This man probably beats more balls than any other two golfers in the world. He practices too much. He'll practice four hours after a round in a hard rain with the temperature 40 degrees and the wind screaming. It's a compulsion with him. He's the kind of single-minded guy who would do almost anything to win.

He's a helluva putter. He scares that hole to death from any distance. He keeps his hands in very close to his body putting.

His swing isn't pretty but it's the most efficient of all the young players. He keeps the club on the same plane through his backswing and downswing.

144

Tom Kite This determined young Texan could fly high before he's done. He has as much determination as anybody out here. He isn't afraid to make major swing changes to become a better player, which is hard to do after you get caught up in the week-to-week pressure of the tour. Right now he's trying mightily to add twenty yards to his tee shots, working with Bob Toski. He and Ben Crenshaw both come from Austin, Texas, and have been quietly intense rivals since they were kids.

Gene Littler In 1972, Gene had cancer surgery. For a while it looked as if he wouldn't live, let alone play golf. The cancer is arrested today.

Anybody who gets cancer is going to get plenty of sympathy. In Gene's case the sentiment was genuine. Everyone liked him *before* he was sick. He's colorless to the public, but around other golfers he's fun and good company. "I drew a big gallery today," he might say. "I was paired with Palmer."

He collects rare old cars—he has a 1924 Rolls Royce—and loves to tinker with them and drive them around.

People think Gene has a great swing, but he doesn't. He has super tempo and gives himself time to make mechanical compensations during his swing.

John Mahaffey Mr. Hogan is high on this young fellow and that's good enough for me. I've helped John a little myself and he's a keen pupil.

He needs to get stronger physically and tougher mentally and he could win a lot of golf tournaments. He's from Texas, and Hogan has counseled him. John says he's trying to develop a better stare, like Hogan's. Hogan has left John's game alone but has built his confidence tremendously.

John is notable among the young players for a lack of cockiness. He obviously has confidence, but he doesn't wear it on his sleeve. He's polite and shows respect for the older players. At first I thought John might be too pleasant a kid to be a big winner. But I don't think so now. He's cutting out that one bad round per tournament that was killing him, and he could be a good one. I hope it doesn't bug him too much that he's blown good chances to win two U.S. Opens.

Roger Maltbie He won back-to-back tournaments as a rookie in 1975 and misplaced his winner's check in a bar after the second one. He's a fun-seeking, refreshing young bachelor whose attitude will let him last for a long time. It was only fitting that he won the tough Memorial Tournament in 1976 by caroming a wild shot off a gallery rope stake to beat Hale Irwin, who didn't speak to him for weeks.

Roger likes people and parties. I hope he doesn't change.

Johnny Miller Young John is the tour's Mr. Clean. He doesn't smoke, drink, cuss, or wink at strange girls. He plays pool—but only in Billy Casper's recreation room.

John has mod blond hair and wears bright mod clothes, and if you didn't know him you might guess he's golf's answer to Joe Namath. Instead he's golf's answer to Jack Armstrong. He's a Mormon like his mentor Casper.

Early in his career it looked as if Johnny might succeed Tommy Aaron as the near-miss king of the tour. He had good chances to win in tournaments like the Masters, but blew them from lack of experience. He got in a playoff on the West Coast and hit a shank. Some players wondered if his stomach was tough enough. But he broke through to win the 1973 U.S. Open at Oakmont with a record-breaking 63 the last day, which just might be the greatest round ever shot, and he's had several terrific streaks since.

He has the temperament to last a long time. He's quiet and hard to rattle, and he doesn't try to do more with a shot than he can bring off without straining.

He's tall but he sits down to the ball well. His takeaway is excellent, but then he moves the club so upright that he breaks his natural plane. He makes the necessary adjustments com-

146

ing down. He's a sneaky long driver. He isn't a spectacular putter, but he can hit his irons so close to the hole that he doesn't have to be.

The only question I have about his future is whether he will have enough endurance. He has to pace his schedule. He says the major tournaments don't mean that much to him, but I wonder.

Bob Murphy He's a cheerful guy and needs to lose about 40 pounds to last out here.

Bob's is an unusual story. He didn't play golf until he was at the University of Florida. He was a scholarship baseball pitcher but hurt his shoulder and took up golf. Three years later he won the NCAA and the U.S. Amateur, and I don't know anybody else who ever developed that fast.

Bob's swing features a long pause at the top. It can throw off his timing. You have to have a lot of strength to hold that club up there like that. Dan Sikes does it, and he's a powerful man. "Murph the Surf" can putt the bottom out of the hole when he has it going.

Bobby Nichols He may have the best deal in golf. He plays on the tour with an exemption as a PGA champion from back before the rules were changed. Then he goes home to Firestone Country Club in Akron, where he's the head pro at about $75,000 a year, plus expenses. The main part of his job is to play golf with the company's top business contacts.

Bobby has the ability to win big purses against top fields. He won the $60,000 first prize in the late Dow Jones Tournament and the $50,000 first prize in the 1973 Westchester Classic.

Bobby's game is very steady. He hits the ball about as far as anyone, especially with the long irons. He loves playing at Firestone, a tough long-iron course. That keeps him sharp for his tour appearances.

147

Arnold Palmer As somebody out here said, Arnold suffers fools more gladly than anybody else in the world. Thousands of people bother him wherever we play, but he is unfailingly courteous. I know Arnold frowns on the edginess of other players and contends that a man isn't truly a superstar until he has learned to tolerate all the annoyances that go with being a hero.

And don't think Arnold isn't still a hero. In many cities he still draws the biggest galleries early in the tournament. He has that magnetic image, and people never count him out. He's still the come-from-behind charger even though he isn't coming from behind much anymore. I don't think he ever did charge that much more than other good players. If you looked it up you'd probably find that he's blown as many tournaments as he's won playing aggressively. But the fans love him for taking gambles and playing dangerously, and he has the flair to make an ordinary shot look more dramatic than it is.

He is highly aware of his galleries. He establishes a rapport with the crowd on the first tee and it builds during a round. He can look into the gallery and give the impression he is making personal contact with everyone in it. I'm guessing that one of his problems in later years has been his weakness for pretty girls. Some of that looking around has to take the sharpness off his concentration.

His galleries have been good for Arnold's game. They make noise and encourage him and that has the twofold effect of inspiring him and distracting his playing partners. What's really difficult is to play in the group in front of him. When he putts out everybody runs to the next hole, even if his partners haven't putted yet. You can be addressing the ball and get the feeling you are about to be trampled by a herd of stampeding buffalo.

Arnold plays to the gallery and loves the attention but he tries to control his fans. He holds up his hands to ask them to

148

wait until everyone has putted, but there isn't that much he can do. The hero-worshippers in his gallery ought to appreciate that somebody has to play along with Arnold to keep his score if nothing else.

Arnold is not above using his gallery as a physical aid. It helps his depth perception to have all those people encircling the green when he's hitting an approach shot and he might even hit at the gallery when it's the intelligent tactic. When people are layered 10 and 12 deep, somebody is going to get in the way of his ball and stop it.

I expect Arnold is going to have a terrible adjustment to make when he has to retire in the next few years. He'll miss being the focus of attention. He has thrived on adulation for so long, I don't see how he could ever live a quiet life out of the limelight. He may go into politics or television.

I don't see how he can last many more years on the tour. He's been struggling for several years, especially with his putting. When he was winning big he would boldly go for the hole on his first putt, confident that if he knocked it well past he could still get down in two. Now he isn't making those second putts, and that costs him confidence on his first putts. He's tried dozens of putters and postures and strokes, but nothing works for long. It's almost sad watching him grope for a quick cure.

His long game has held up better. His swing is slower and smoother than it used to be but it will never be called classic. He changed it mainly because he has hip trouble and is avoiding surgery. Arnold plays with an extremely weak grip and a closed clubface—it's a muscleman's swing. His approach has always been to overpower the ball. He is the perfect example of a hitter as opposed to a swinger.

When Arnold is gone, the rest of us players will be the poorer for it. More than any other player, he has made the tour and the game grow in the last twenty years. There's no telling how much money he's made for me by boosting golf's popularity. He's probably the most famous athlete ever. After all, Babe Ruth didn't have the advantages of the modern media coverage. I appreciate what Arnold has done for the tour, and everybody out here should.

Over all, Arnold is popular with the other players. He's congenial off the course, and an earthy, approachable guy. The few players who don't like him don't carry their dislike far. "I'm not crazy about him," says Dan Sikes, who broke in when Arnold did. "But when he's in contention I find myself damn near pulling for him. The guy projects something that nobody else does."

Jerry Pate A cocky kid who might be every bit as good as he thinks he is. All he did in his rookie year in 1976 was win the U.S. and Canadian Opens! He's typical of the new breed of college products who come out on the tour ready to win. It used to take a man five years to adjust to the tour. It takes the Jerry Pates about five weeks.

Pate has an enviable swing. He takes the club straight back from the ball and brings it straight through at impact. He has a shoulder turn he could sell for a fortune. His tempo is truly remarkable—he's in complete control of his swing from start to finish and never seems to force a shot.

All he has to do is keep working at the game and not fall out of an airplane, and he could be a great one.

Gary Player Lack of dedication has never been Gary's problem. He has done more with his natural ability than anyone else playing the game today. He works harder at golf than the rest of us—as he is always telling anyone who will listen, especially the writers.

Gary is a little man and he's tremendously proud of his superior physical condition. He runs and lifts weights and eats health foods. That's all well and good, but I get tired of hearing him brag about it. So what if he has the most perfect bowel movements on the tour?

He reminds me of a man who takes too many vitamin pills. He figures that if one is good for him, then a hundred will be a hundred times as good for him. Also Gary is a very shrewd individual. When he is pushing bananas and having them delivered to the locker room by the crateful, you can bet he has a good endorsement deal going with a banana company.

I have nothing against people like Gary who don't drink or smoke. I do resent them telling me that that's how I should live. Gary makes a lot of other players mad with his sanctimonious preachings about clean living. He likes to go on as though he's the only athlete on the tour. He's always pointing at somebody's paunch with great disdain. He overdoes it.

Weightlifting and developing all those muscles may have hurt Gary's golf some. Lifting heavy weights can shorten your muscles and tighten your back and shoulders. The golf swing is a long, stretching action. You need all the suppleness you can get to make a big turn. Lifting weights can make you as taut as a banjo string, and that isn't going to help your golf swing. Gary has great coordination and doesn't need that extra muscular development he gets from lifting weights.

His style setting up to the ball is very rigid, very tense. He is overdeveloped in the forearms and shoulders, and those muscles are extremely firm. He looks like a mechanical man. From that kind of address position it is awfully difficult for him to create the freedom of motion that marks a great golf swing. Jack Nicklaus and Sam Snead are very firm in the hands at address, but Player is firm all the way up to his shoulders. I have always believed Gary was trying to copy Ben Hogan's swing, but Hogan never set up to the ball that rigidly.

Like Hogan, Gary has always fought a tendency to hook the ball wildly. He still can regress into spells where he hooks the ball clear off the course. Gary used to misunderstand what Hogan was doing, as almost everybody does. He thought Hogan was fanning the clubface open with his arms on his takeaway. If you study pictures of Mr. Hogan closely, you will see that he did not fan the clubface open with the arms—he set it on his swing plane quickly with his hands. He cocked his wrists quickly on his takeaway and kept them cocked all the way through his swing until he was in the impact zone.

Gary used to roll the clubface open with his arms and then roll it shut through the ball, which caused him to hook. Like Hogan, Gary starts his downswing with a strong lateral move onto his left side and the club drops a good foot and a half from its backswing plane onto a much flatter downswing plane. This flat downswing plane holds the clubface on the target line longer, but you have to let your hands release faster, and that opens up the danger of the big hook.

Gary is one of the few players capable of experimenting with his swing and putting the club in different positions when he wants to, trying to determine which is the best. He realized he was fanning the clubface open with his arms and then rolling it shut, and he pretty much stopped doing it.

Gary solicits far too much advice on the practice tee—I've seen him taking a lesson at the U.S. Open from a hot dog vendor—but he filters it out. He knows when somebody has spotted something that can help him and when the advice is meaningless.

You can't see your own swing. Gary uses a bystander as a mirror to check his action but he doesn't get confused by conflicting tips the way most pros would. He still lapses into spates of hooking, but he usually has the problem under control. He's a fine student of the game and I enjoy debating theory with him.

His weakness is the finesse shot. It's difficult for him to play a three-quarter shot, again mainly because he is so rigid at address. Once he has made that strong coil on his backswing, he has to turn all his power loose right from the top of his swing. Gary can't take a 4-wood from 175 yards and put a long, easy swing on it. For him a three-quarter swing is choking down on the grip an inch and a half and still going at it full bore.

Obviously, Gary's power approach works for him. He hasn't won all the major championships with a lousy method. But he can't be classified with a Hogan or a Tommy Bolt when you're comparing the great shotmakers.

Gary's putting has to be better than average, but here too his rigidity must work against him. You have to be relaxed to putt consistently well, and Gary is tense. He makes a lot of putts out of sheer determination and hard practice. I've seen him stand on a practice green for an hour in 100-degree heat sinking one-foot putts. I asked him what he was doing and he said he was grooving a stroke and gaining confidence from seeing and hearing the ball rattle into the hole. That's how seriously he takes this game.

Gary has become suspicious about American galleries since the trouble he had with a few spectators who called him a racist a couple of years ago when South Africa, his homeland, was prominent in the news because of its apartheid policies. Gary's life was even threatened, and he played the Masters one year surrounded by law officers. These agitators certainly didn't know anything about golf, and I don't think they knew much about Gary's politics. By South African standards he's a flaming liberal. Gary spoke out at home for integrated sports opportunities for blacks when it was risky for him to take a stand. Certainly he enjoys a favored position as an international golf star, but he nevertheless took a chance of having his travel privileges revoked, at the least. The government over there doesn't tolerate criticism, even from celebrities.

He invited Lee Elder to South Africa to play in exhibitions and tournaments with him, and while it may have been a grandstand play to get American radicals off his back, it served to help integrate athletics in South Africa, and that in turn is serving to help integrate the society as a whole.

Gary all but stopped playing in the Northeastern part of the United States because of the fan abuse. Fortunately, it has just about died and he is being accepted for what he is: a tremendous, dedicated golfer who puts out a little phony baloney but no more than most people want to hear.

Chi Chi Rodriguez Cheech and I are supposed to be enemies. I hate to ruin a good story, but we've always been friends with the brief exception of one well-publicized incident that caused some hard feelings. Well, actually I literally was going to kill the little peckerwood that time.

When Cheech first came to the tour from Puerto Rico we traveled together. He stayed at my house and we did a lot of partying together at night on the road. Cheech was single then. He since married a beautiful girl from Hawaii—Iwalani, who was a native dancer and who is about twice his size. We still play practice rounds together and occasionally have dinner together.

Our temporary falling out started with the 1970 Kemper Open. We were paired in a twosome on the final day. I had a chance to win the tournament and Chi Chi didn't. The tournament had been delayed a day and we were playing 36 holes. That's a long time to spend with anyone under pressure on a golf course, let alone a Chi Chi Rodriguez.

During the morning round he was a complete gentleman. But during the afternoon round he started clowning around and it bothered me. I was just a shot away from the lead and was edgy anyway. At the fifth hole he made a birdie and did a dance and plunked his straw hat down over the hole to keep the ball from getting out. It's one of the routines he's done for years. I let that pass because the gallery, which had grown steadily in size, enjoyed it and it wasn't interfering with my play.

Then at the sixth tee he went through a stand-up comedy routine using his old lines about Puerto Rican power—beans and rice. The fans laughed and he drove down the right side of the fairway. I prepared to hit my drive and the crowd was still laughing, so I backed away and started over. Again I got ready to shoot and the gallery was still laughing. Finally I decided to be done with it and I drove the ball way left, left of the bunker on that side of the fairway.

I arrived at the ball in the rough and started trying to figure a way to get it up near the front of the green so I might chip up and save a par. Nobody was paying any attention to me. I was asking people to move so I could have a shot but they were looking the other way and laughing. I walked up a little hill to see what was going on and there was Chi Chi—whose ball was on the other side of the fairway—standing in the near bunker with a rake, acting like he was Willie Mays with a baseball bat. I moved the people and didn't say anything to him, but went back and hit my shot just off the green 30 feet from the hole.

I walked up on the green to see whether it was wet or hard or what, and Chi Chi was talking to the fans and making a commotion. I called him over and asked him if he kindly would stop his goddam clowning until I had played my shot. I told him I didn't care what he did after I had finished the hole but in the meantime I was trying to win a tournament and needed a little courtesy. He bitched and moaned. I chipped to three feet from the hole and now he was yelling and screaming and so were the fans, because they guessed what I said to him. We both proceeded to miss our short putts.

We went to the seventh tee and the crowd was all over me. And Chi Chi refused to play with me!

An official came out and told him that if he didn't want to play with me he would have to go into the clubhouse, and if he wanted to finish the round he would have to cool his clowning act. We played the seventh hole and I made a birdie 2, and on the eighth hole I made a birdie 3 and tied for the lead.

We teed off on the ninth hole and walked down the fairway—and Chi Chi started an argument. I was trying to get ready to hit my second shot and he challenged me to a fistfight on the spot. I told him there damned sure was going to be a fight but it was going to be at the end of the round.

155

I missed a short birdie putt on nine and then made a good saving par on ten. I knocked the ball over the green with my second shot but chipped back six inches from the hole. Walking to the eleventh tee, Chi Chi announced, "The black hat made another easy par."

The steam was billowing out of my ears. The eleventh is a par-3 with water around the green. I put it in the water and wound up making a 6 on a short hole.

As mad as I was, I didn't really get furious until the end of the tournament. I had a chance to tie for the championship with a twelve-foot putt on the eighteenth, which I missed. Then I thought about what that triple bogey on the eleventh hole did to me, and a four-alarm rage swept through my veins. I went to find Chi Chi in the locker room just to sort of knock his brains out. I'm sure I could have killed him, the frame of mind I was in. Officials kept me away from him and got him out of there.

But that's the only real argument Chi Chi and I have ever had in twelve years on the tour. He never apologized. He seemed to want to apologize, but he never did, and it blew over.

He forgot that you can carry the clowning bit too far, that's all. The following year Chi Chi missed the top 60 and decided he'd better concentrate more on his golf and less on show biz, and he won at Dallas and has played much better.

Chi Chi always could hit a lot of good shots, even when he was clowning, but when he clowned he also hit a lot of bad shots. He hasn't quit clowning altogether, which is fine. The tour needs a bright personality like his. But it's a question of timing. You don't joke with the gallery when another player is trying to play a shot. The damned game is tough enough without that kind of hot-dogging for a distraction.

Chi Chi has always wanted everyone to like him. He comes from a background of poverty and wants to give something back to everyone in golf. He has a heart as big as the moon. He does many things for charity in Puerto Rico and has never pulled up his roots there. You have to admire his motivation.

His game matured at about the same time his attitude improved. He used to throw everything he had into every tee shot, trying to make up for his lack of size and give the fans a thrill, and he got to where he was moving his head violently on his backswing and throwing his whole swing out of whack. He has eased off enough to regain his control.

He has a phenomenal touch with the short irons. I've seen him take a dozen balls during a practice round and arrange them in a variety of the worst lies you can imagine in a sand trap, and hit all of them close to the hole. He'll take a stance almost standing on his head and slice the ball out of a buried lie under the back lip of a trap. He says he learned those sand shots growing up on the beach in Puerto Rico.

Cheech recently changed his looks by buying a hairpiece that fits down the middle of his head. Unfortunately it looks just like a stray divot.

J. C. Snead Seldom confused with his uncle Sam. But he can play some. He's a strapping country boy who can move it off the tee. His tempo isn't as good as Sam's (whose is?) but it's good.

Carlyle, as he prefers to be called, didn't turn pro until he gave up on baseball at the age of 22. He was a good hitting outfielder in the Washington Senator chain and got as high as AA ball.

Carlyle had never played with his uncle before coming out on the tour. Sam made one big change in his swing. He taught him to keep his right elbow in close to his body so his arms could follow his shoulder turn.

Carlyle's ambition is to win the U.S. Open for Sam, who never broke his long jinx in the Open.

Carlyle is a little bit of a wild man. He has a temper that can go off like Mount Vesuvius and he likes to gamble.

Sam Snead This could be the greatest natural athlete of all time. Who else has ever been at the top of his sport at 60-plus years of age?

He was a born holer. He's won 84 PGA tournaments, more than anybody else in history—and he's still capable of winning. If he could make his share of fifteen-foot putts, he could beat Jack Nicklaus. Sam is long off the tee even today, and he can hit you just about any golf shot you want. He has so much sensitivity in his hands, he can feel the hair on them.

Sam has a self-developed swing that is the best going in my estimation. His tempo is classic. He isn't perfect mechanically—he doesn't play with a square clubface and his leg action is a little rigid—but over all his swing is tops.

One reason Sam has been able to play so well for so long is that he has a big swing. It isn't as big as it used to be, but it was so big to start with, he hasn't lost much distance with age. His suppleness is unbelievable. He makes a beautiful full shoulder turn, a great turn. Sam likes to make you think he doesn't do a lot of exercises, but don't you believe it. He's always doing stretching exercises.

I've always thought Sam is double-jointed, which accounts for some of his flexibility. He can keep one foot on the floor and kick the top of a doorway with the other foot. And he can reach down and pick his ball out of the cup without bending his knees.

Sam was born with his limberness and coordination, but he works to keep in shape. He does hundreds of sit-ups every week to stretch his muscles and keep his tummy hard. He figures he's hit almost two million golf shots counting practice. He's some kind of specimen.

Sam has some memorable mental images of his swing. Somebody asked him now he maintained such super tempo. "I try to feel oily," he said. When he was asked how he hooked the ball, he said, "I think hook."

158

He is such a gifted athlete that he doesn't have to worry about how to hold the club and set his feet for a hook. He just feels it, sees it in his mind, and does it. Sam has done nothing but play golf all his life—well, almost nothing—and it's second nature to him.

Sam knows more about the golf swing than people give him credit for. He's no dumb country boy about this game. He's always been a teaching pro and he figures he's given more lessons than a lot of big-name teachers who can't break 80. He has taught himself, but he can analyze other people's swings quickly and not confuse them with a lot of double-talk.

His primary weakness has been his putting late in his career. He's played so long, his nerves are gone on the greens. He has a terminal case of the Yips.

Sam seemed to have the Yips whipped using a croquet-style stroke between his legs. But the style was outlawed. I thought it was pretty ridiculous to ban it simply because it didn't look conventional. On that basis you would have to outlaw quite a few swings with the driver on this tour. Who in hell cares what you look like if you can get the job done? And Sam was getting the job done. I would guess he'd be winning two or three tournaments a year if he could putt croquet-style.

He's adapted a sidewinder style now, with both feet on the same side of the putting line but still facing the hole. This way he uses the big muscles of his shoulders and arms instead of the smaller, twitchier muscles of the wrists and hands. He has some confidence in this method. He says he can putt the orthodox way in practice almost as well as he ever did, but under pressure he can't sink a thing.

It takes guts to change from the conventional approach as Sam did. You have to have a helluva vivid imagination and you have to retrain your thinking and muscular patterns. That's how great an athlete Sam is. He can do anything he sets his mind to. He could have been a superstar in any sport he chose—football, basketball, baseball. I'm glad he chose golf; he can last longer here.

Sam's personality is natural, too. He is leery of strangers. Sam grew up in the backwoods of West Virginia and worked hard for his money, and he is slow to part with it. Fred Corcoran, who used to manage Sam, jokes that Sam is the only man to make a million dollars and save two million. The stories about Sam burying his fortune in tomato cans down home are exaggerated, but he doesn't go around giving it away.

He can be aloof to people he doesn't know. I've seen him look right past a man who was asking him about the golf balls he uses. The man asked him three times, thinking Sam hadn't heard him, and Sam never indicated he existed—Sam isn't hard of hearing. But if he trusts you, you see a completely different person, and you're lucky. Sam can be a tremendously warm person. Unbeknownst to the public, he has helped many young players with their swings when they asked him.

He is a funny story-teller around the locker room if he's with the handful of players he really likes. He tells stories in that hill-country accent that fractures my body. I remember one about a young high society lady who came to him for a lesson at the Greenbrier. Sam said she was about the only hopeless case he has seen in golf. She took some practice swings as Sam cringed, and Sam noticed something pink peeking out of her blouse. Before he could do anything she swung several more times, and out onto the ground popped a falsie. Sam says it bounced a few times, rolled in a couple of pretty little circles, and stopped smack in front of them. The lady was blushing and about to burst into tears, and after a long and painful silence Sam said, "That's okay, honey, just leave it there and we'll tee up on it." She gave up the game.

I was lucky enough to get to know Sam when he coached the Ryder Cup team I played on in Britain in 1969. It was a long trip and we were thrown together frequently. I developed a strong affection and respect for the man. I learned that Sam knew a libraryful about this game. And I learned that he has class. Sam always eats dinner in a jacket and tie. He'll shower and change when he comes off the course at 2 P.M. if he suspects he'll be eating out later.

A good many of the younger players on the tour could take a lesson from Sam. Guys like Grier Jones go out to eat in a nice restaurant looking like war refugees. They're making a hundred thousand a year and go out in public looking almost like bums. Not Sam. He may be from the country but he knows he has a reputation to live up to. And what a reputation.

Dave Stockton He has a horrible swing, but he gets away with it. Dave hurt his back water-skiing as a youngster and the injury affected his golf swing. He can't make a good move. He aims far to the right and comes over the top of all his shots. He finishes on the wrong side of the ball and is lucky to drive it 250 yards.

But he recognizes his deficiencies and has the guts to play around them. He never quits.

He's a great scrambler—he can get it up and down out of a ballwasher. He frequently complains about his putting; that drives other pros up the wall because they can't putt half as well as Stockton at his worst. Dan Sikes says Stockton is going to get killed one of these days saying he's a bad putter.

Dave is a good guy but overly ambitious about money. He thinks it's the end-all.

Lee Trevino I'm afraid Lee's attitude is getting worse. A couple of years ago I thought he was the greatest thing that could have happened to golf. He entertained people without bothering his playing partners—he isn't a showoff type like Chi Chi Rodriguez or Hubert Green—and he played over 30 tournaments a year to help the sponsors. But Lee overextended himself with outside activities and his personality began to suffer. He refused to sign autographs if he was in a hurry and hadn't played well. He knocked courses and dropped out of tournaments.

This is a different Lee Trevino. I don't think the man has basically changed, I think he is just setting too fast a pace and it's catching up with him. You can't do everything he's trying to do and stay happy all the time. Lee is a genuinely funny man. He's quick with spontaneous one-liners and delivers them with a fine sense of timing. Once a lady was oohing and aahing over his shots on the practice tee and he spun around and yelped, "What did you expect from a U.S. Open champion, lady—ground balls? Lately he seems to be repeating his one-liners, too tired to get off fresh ones. He chatters all the time but seems to be doing it in an effort to relax.

It's understandable that Lee would try to do too much too soon. He came up the back way and nobody did him any favors. He was a poor Mexican in Texas, where a Mexican can rank below a black on the social scale. He had all sorts of problems getting his PGA card to play the tour.

Lee is older than the tour guide lists him, by three or four years, and he was around 30 when he finally came on the tour. I was one of the first people to learn who he was. I was paired with him during the U.S. Open at Baltusrol in New Jersey in 1967. I rode to the course with a friend, who asked me if I'd ever heard of my playing partner. I said no.

Lee was extremely quiet and nervous then. It was his first major tournament and I guess his first real national test, and his wife had spent the family savings to enter him in the Open. He hit the ball beautifully. On the fourth hole I walked over to my friend in the gallery and said, "We may not know who this cat is but he can play like gangbusters." Trevino shot 68 that day and finished fifth in the Open. He wasn't an unknown much longer.

He had the same unorthodox swing he has now. He set up

162

to the left and then blocked the shot—didn't let himself turn over on the ball and hit it left. His legwork was tremendous. He obviously had fought a hook earlier in his career and found a way to play that made it almost impossible for him to hook. He can repeat his action, and if he's smart he'll never change it. He had all the trick shots he'd developed working as a driving-range pro and he could putt the bottom out of the hole.

Since then he has put together a great record and become a big crowd favorite. He has never pretended to be someone he isn't. He kiddingly calls me "Bad Boy." He still lives in El Paso and the people who work for him are old friends. I'm sure he could get more dynamic business associates but Lee would rather reward people who stood by him during the slow years. One young man who travels with him a lot at Lee's expense is an old pal who is crippled—Lee took him on as soon as he could afford it.

Lee's trouble is that he's almost too generous. He tries to do too much and so runs himself down and gets irritable. He has to pace himself better or he isn't going to last, not with the kind of life he's led all these years. He loves golf more than anyone else out here I think, and it would be a shame for him and the game if he doesn't slow down and let the old Lee Trevino shine through.

Tom Weiskopf Tom has always had the mechanical game to challenge Nicklaus, but you have to wonder if he'll ever grow up. Sometimes I think that when he reaches 50, people still will be saying what wonderful potential he has. If he gets his head on straight he could win four and five tournaments a year for a long time. He's getting better, slowly. He worships Nicklaus and Nicklaus counsels him about settling down.

Weiskopf is an Ohio boy like Nicklaus and I think he suffered for quite a while from people comparing him with Jack. He didn't have the early national amateur experience that

163

Jack enjoyed and it wasn't a fair comparison. When Nicklaus turned pro he was ready to win. When Weiskopf turned pro he was way behind Jack. He tried to hit the ball farther than Jack and forgot that distance isn't worth anything without direction.

Weiskopf has had a hard time learning that winning golf is hard work and nobody gets all good breaks. He's spoiled and conceited and thinks everything should go exactly the way he wants it to. He reminds me of a kid I used to play marbles with. When he couldn't win he'd pick up his marbles and go home.

I've never wanted to have anything to do with Weiskopf because he can go weeks without speaking to you. You can say hello in the locker room and he'll walk by you without a word. He did it to Bob Goalby one day and Goalby was going to break him in half. Goalby may be the toughest man out here and has a ready temper. He can handle all cases. Weiskopf doesn't know how close he came to being clobbered.

Weiskopf is very moody. I can sympathize with him there because I'm very moody too. But his moodiness turns inward and mine comes out. Weiskopf broods where I just let it all hang out and then forget it. My way is healthier. When he is up, he is way up. But when he's down he's morose. He has great desire and expects more of himself than he gets. He realizes how awesome his potential is and knows that he hasn't lived up to it often enough, and that has to be depressing to him.

He has to reconcile himself to life going against him now and then—be more realistic. When he doesn't do well he has to act decently to people even if he doesn't feel like it. The sun does not rise and set for just Tom Weiskopf.

He's beginning to learn that he has to work at the game if he's going to be a top player. I see him on the practice range more often. Mechanically he has it all. He has the best swing I've ever seen. He can drive the ball about as long and straight as anybody and is a tremendous long-iron player. He can putt

164

well enough to win. His tempo is very smooth. He's taller than any great player yet—six-feet-three—but swings in good balance.

A bad shot doesn't upset him as much as it used to. In the past he could let one poor shot ruin an entire round. If his attitude continues to improve, watch out, Jack.

MANAGERS

Mark McCormack has survived quite lavishly without Nicklaus. He's still the king of the 20 percenters, the agents. He hates being called an agent: he says he's a business manager. He may be the biggest man in golf. He made it big with Palmer and now has top stars from other sports, and even composer Burt Bacharach. He can make or break a tournament. It's some machine. It's too big for me. I never signed with McCormack because I figured he would never have time for me.

I am not that fond of the man. I don't know him well, but my impressions are not favorable. He likes to control a person's every move. He tells you what to do and when and how to do it, and I am not one to sit still for that. If he wants you to fly across the country to be in New York City for a speaking engagement next Tuesday, you fly across the country and speak.

He tells his players what to say to the public and the press.

You know, be sure and be nice to everybody and stay away from controversy. When the players were feuding with the PGA officers and threatening to start their own tour, Arnold Palmer didn't take a stand. I think he had some things he wanted to say—I think he was sympathetic toward the PGA because his father had been a loyal club pro—but he didn't say them. I'm guessing that McCormack told him to keep quiet so he wouldn't jeopardize any of his rich contracts.

That isn't my speed. Neither is letting a manager take a piece of what I win on the tour. McCormack and most of the rest of the agents who have followed him into our business want anywhere from 15 to 25 percent of your winnings. If he isn't ready to guarantee me about $100,000 a year in outside income, he can forget it. He doesn't do anything to help me win prize money. I don't mind his taking a share of any new income he brings in, but let him get off his butt and go earn his keep.

I turned managers down for years, all of them. I don't play golf for the money, I play because I enjoy the game. Money isn't my god, and I pray that it never will be. I can make $2,000 a week playing money games in Palm Springs. I've always contended that if a player hasn't won half a dozen major championships he doesn't need a manager. He just needs a lawyer and a tax man.

I threw in with Ed Barner when I had the lawsuit going against the PGA. He had been after me to sign and he was helpful during a difficult time.

Ed didn't know beans about golf at the time and still can barely tell the difference between a bird on the golf course and a bird in the bush. He came out of show business—he used to manage singer Trini Lopez. He's a Mormon and his first golfer was Billy Casper, who later got him together with Johnny Miller. Ed makes a wholesome appearance, but he can be a tough negotiator.

I told Ed I'd try it with him on a six-month trial basis, and

167

I'm still with him. We have an unusual agreement. He doesn't touch my prize money; he gets no percentage of it. We negotiated long and hard on that point and I held firm. I know it made some of the young hot rocks in his stable mad when they found out he was getting a cut of their winnings but not of mine. Hell, I wasn't even a college graduate and here I'd driven a smarter bargain than they had. I came out of the Graduate School of Hustle.

The other point of contention that Ed and I argued loud and long was whether he should get a percentage of contracts I already had. I was adamant that I hadn't needed him to get those deals and I didn't need him taking a cut of them. I didn't have that many deals, but it was the principle.

We finally compromised that he would get a percentage of new business he brought in or of improvements in contracts he renegotiated. That's really why players have managers, I feel—to negotiate. I hate to dicker with anybody. I'm not good at it and I don't like it. I can let him do the dickering. That doesn't mean I want him highjacking somebody to pay me more than the relationship is worth. I've never been greedy. If I'm offered a decent buck, I'll take it and not complain. I've made that clear to Ed and I keep in touch with all the negotiations.

I'm not trying to hold anybody up, but I hate to find out that a company is paying me less than it's paying some young kid who isn't playing as well as I am. That's what happened on my Munsingwear deal.

I have been with Munsingwear for a long time. I started at $1,000 a year and worked up slowly but steadily. Then after I'd been out here a dozen years, I found out that some guys who can't carry my shag bag were making more than I am. If I feel that I am being taken advantage of, I feel justified in taking advantage right back.

Munsingwear raised me to $5,000 and that helped heal the wound, but I should have been getting that from the beginning. That's the kind of difficulty I like to turn over to a manager. He gets paid to be an SOB. But I want to know when he's being nasty and why. I don't want him pressuring to raise contracts that are equitable.

Remember the big squabble between Lee Trevino and his first manager, Bucky Woy? They had themselves a pretty good fight and then Lee pulled away from Bucky. I think the big reason was that Bucky pushed and pushed for more money on Lee's contracts when Lee was well satisfied with them, and Lee saw that Bucky was ruining some good relationships and didn't like it a bit.

The Dodge deal was the straw that broke Woy's back, I understand. Lee did a series of commercials for Dodge and got a pretty good piece of change, something like $30,000. Lee was happy. But Lee wasn't getting any residuals from Dodge and Woy thought he ought to be. Woy tried to high-pressure Dodge, and Dodge told him to get lost. Then Lee told Bucky to get lost, and Lee got his own deal back with Dodge. Lee is capable of negotiating his own contracts, which he generally does these days.

I don't think a manager should hold a figure over a company's head. Most managers try to force these companies to the point where the golf pro is making more than the president of the company, and all that does is make the manager a pimp who has overpriced his merchandise. What Trevino realized is that if you are a really hot item, the deals are going to fall in your lap. You don't have to go out high-pressuring people to get them. If you're not a really hot item, you don't need a manager at all—not to book you six $2,500 exhibitions a year. It can be an ego massage to have a manager making your plane and hotel reservations and sending in your tournament entries, but you don't need him for those chores.

I can see winning a major tournament and maybe hiring a manager for a year to try to generate everything possible out of it. You will have a lot of offers that he can help you sort out.

You're an attraction for a while, then the public cools on you fast. Look at Gay Brewer or Orville Moody. They needed a manager for a year after they won a big one, but they don't need one today.

A player should make sure the manager cannot cost him money. I think Ed Barner has the fairest approach for the players, because he at least guarantees you he will not cost you money. He has to get out and hump to make both of us money; he can't sit back and peck at my winnings. I don't know any other manager who works on that basis.

Of course, you don't actually come out even in that case. The player is out the time he spent doing extra exhibitions or whatever it was Barner arranged. You usually do these extra things toward the end of the season, and that time is valuable to me to relax and be with my family.

Ed is big on foreign travel. He'll book you in Japan—or Siberia if he can work it out. Well, I've been playing long enough to know I don't want to put in any extra weeks unless I can average $5,000 a week plus expenses. It just isn't worth it to me.

The main reason you go abroad is to promote equipment or clothing you endorse in the foreign countries. Japan is a hot spot. Those folks are crazy on golf. Even I am a hero over there. I have a clothing contract with Toray Industries in Japan for $10,000 a year. All I have to do is wear their clothes when I play in Japan or in a television match here that will be aired in Japan. My logo on the clothes is a cute little giraffe. I'm not sure what that's supposed to mean. The giraffe has its back arched and its mouth wide open.

I also do promotional work for William Grant & Sons whiskey, both in Japan and the United States. I never say I drink it—I'm a vodka man myself. I do ads that say "Join this contest to try to beat Dave Hill with your score on such-and-such a course using your handicap." It isn't actually an endorsement. I get $15,000 a year for that and for playing an occasional pro-am.

It often astonishes people who think they know me as an impetuous loner that I like playing customer golf. I really do. Playing tournament golf for a living demands so much of you physically and mentally that it's exhausting. After eighteen holes of heavy concentration—figuring and planning every shot, trying never to let myself get sloppy—I'm ready to collapse. When I play customer golf I can relax and enjoy the game.

I'm not trying to protect anything and I just go out there and look at the hole and let 'er fly. It's amazing how much easier the game can be when you're able to relax like that. I can hit better golf shots playing for funsies than I can playing in a tournament, because I'm not afraid of anything. I enjoy that.

I don't mind playing with hackers at all. I love to play with people who have a sense of humor and can kid me when I make a bad shot and laugh at their own mistakes. The game was originally meant to be fun—I don't know where we went so wrong. Now we line up a putt for five minutes, miss it, and agonize as if we're waiting to be nailed to a cross. When I don't have to post a low score I can have all kinds of fun on the golf course.

I think I'm friendly with my amateur playing partners. I encourage them to let it all hang out. They don't have to treat me like a big-shot golf pro and stand back and be quietly respectful when I'm shooting. I'm just another guy swinging at a golf ball, a little better than most is all.

I play customer golf with presidents and executives of big companies, men who are much more successful than I am. If I can talk with them and help them with their game and enable them to relax and forget their problems for just three minutes, I take a lot of pleasure in it. Busy business people need to play golf, look at the birds, soak up the sunshine, have a few laughs, get some exercise. Too many of them don't.

I play every year in an outing with an important company president. The first couple of times I played with him he had to make half a dozen phone calls before we teed off and a half

171

dozen more between nines, and when we got in he couldn't stay around for a drink: he had to hurry back to check on his business. He was a very worried man. On the course he was up tight and didn't hit many decent shots.

Since then, that man has learned to relax at golf, and I think the experience has taught him to relax at life. Now he doesn't rush around making phone calls and stewing all the time. He has fun on the course and plays much better. He'll stay for a drink or two afterward and he might even go to dinner with me. Instead of being upset by a bad shot now, he can laugh at it and go on to make a good shot. Helping him learn to relax and enjoy life more gives me a good feeling.

It always astounds me that some of these powerful executives almost worship golf pros. Many of them play golf—they might have started playing to entertain clients at a fancy club they joined on the expense account—and they like associating with golfers. I'm glad they do, because these men have a lot to do with the boom on the tour. They talk their companies into sponsoring golf telecasts even though our audience ratings don't approach the ratings for sports like football. They know other decision-makers watch golf on television. Big companies run some of our best tournaments. It's almost impossible for a community to underwrite a tour event in today's economy.

Playing customer golf can gain you valuable contacts for future deals. I've been playing public relations golf for the Glick Iron & Metal Company in my home state of Michigan since 1966, and it's been a rewarding relationship that has grown into a sponsorship arrangement for me. The company guarantees me a minimum income each year. I turn over my prize money to the people there and they pay me a salary and invest the rest. They're giving me security in an insecure sport. I'm not enough of a businessman to understand all the advantages of our deal, which probably is unique on the tour. I know I make out much better at income tax time.

Playing customer golf for Glick a couple of weeks each summer has helped educate me as a human being, helped me get along better with people. I meet people more easily and understand them better. I mix better and feel that I belong, whereas before I didn't. Many pros don't like customer golf; I enjoy it and appreciate what it's done for me.

I resist the temptation to play customer golf or exhibitions during the weeks I'm competing. I want to concentrate on the tournament at hand and rest some early in the week. You could do those appearances every Monday and Tuesday if you wanted to. My rate is $3,500 a day. That isn't much compared to Nicklaus, Trevino, and Palmer, who are up around $15,000 a day, but it isn't a bad day's wages either. I play a round of golf, have dinner and check out.

We're lucky to have all this extra money available to us out here on tour. I suppose I make almost $100,000 a year on the off-course deals I've mentioned, not counting bonuses or royalties. Lee Trevino probably makes that much every year on his Faultless contract alone. If you can play this game, your prize money will just be the tip of your financial iceberg.

I have Ed Barner screen the deals before I go into them. No pro should take every money-making proposition that comes along. Several dozen pros on the tour wear caps with a big Amana label on the front for about 50 bucks a week. I find it offensive. They lose their individualism. They can't take the silly things off if they're being interviewed on television, which drives the TV producers buggy because millions of viewers can't see their faces. George Archer even signed out of Amana, Iowa, as if it were his home town. He lives in California. If we're going to wear big commercial labels on our caps, the next thing you know we'll have labels on the seats of our pants. Pretty soon we'll look like Indianapolis 500 racing cars all festooned with advertisements.

Overcommercialism could ruin golf if we aren't careful. Fred Corcoran, the best promoter the game has ever seen, got

173

out of managing players not long ago after some dismaying adventures trying to satisfy their greed. He says the players are forgetting about building a good image for the game and thinking too much about building their pocketbooks. He says he always hears the jingle of the cash register in the background today. That's why the managers can't be allowed to take over the game.

EQUIPMENT

You know the advertisements. "Joe Gluck Wins Tarpaper Open Playing Whippersnapper Clubs." Ten million weekend golfers are supposed to read about the pros using one brand or another and run right out and buy a set of clubs. Same with golf balls.

A big part of golf's spectator appeal is the fan's ability to identify with the pro. The fan plays the game himself. It isn't like pro football; how many pro football fans do you know who have played pro football or would be stupid enough to want to? The golf fan has faced the same lonely challenges the star has, and the fan can get the same gratifying results from time to time. The golf fan often believes that what is good for the pro is good for him. He wants the same equipment the pro has. But the weekend player is frequently misled by the pros and the manufacturers.

I'm as guilty as the next guy. I represented the Ram Corporation for years and was supposed to play Ram clubs and balls, but everybody on the tour knew I was playing the Titleist ball. I'm sure the company realized all along I wasn't playing the Ram ball, but nobody ever gave me any static. I appreciate that. The people at Ram realize that a pro is going to play the ball he knows he personally can get the most from. Consistency is the big priority to the pro. He wants to know that if he puts eight identical swings on a full 7-iron shot the ball will go 155 yards all eight times. Not 153 or 157, but 155. Every time. Titleist has always been the big favorite on the tour because it was the most consistent ball. It didn't go farther than all the other balls, but it consistently went the same distance on the same trajectory. If one ball in a dozen does a funny trick it can cost you a tournament.

I never felt bad about endorsing one ball but playing another. That sounds hypocritical coming from Dave Hill, but it isn't at all. Here's why. I get all the golf balls I want, free, from whatever company makes the ball I want to play, no matter if I'm on another company's payroll. If I put a horrible swing on the ball, which doesn't happen too often, and slice the ball in half, I just reach in the bag and pull out another one at no charge. The average weekend player isn't so fortunate. He spends over a dollar on a ball, and if he cuts it, he's lost an expensive item. The average player should use a Surlyn-covered ball because it won't cut and he can play an entire round with it if he doesn't hit it in the water or somebody's watermelon patch. Ram came out with the first Surlyn ball several years ago and I think it's the best ball in the world for the weekend golfer. I've given it to my partners in pro-ams and they love it. They'll beat up a Titleist in three holes until it looks like it's been through the Civil War. I could play Titleist and recommend Ram to the average player with a clear conscience. When Titleist changed its dimple size I switched to the Hogan ball. The majority of players on tour plays the Hogan ball today.

I heard a funny story once about Bert Yancey when he was

representing PGA Victor. A big PGA executive had walked out on the course to follow Bert and tell him he'd meet him after the round to discuss a new contract. Bert was making a bundle of money to play PGA stuff. The PGA man went to the hole Bert was playing and stopped halfway up the fairway to wait for him. Bert happened to drive the ball over that way and it rolled dead at the PGA man's feet. The man looked down, and on the ball it said Titleist. Bert lost the contract.

PGA apparently is one company that insists its players use the equipment they endorse.

A round little man named Eddie Darrell used to be paid by the manufacturers to run a weekly check on the players and see if they actually were playing the equipment they were getting paid to play. He had many intricate ploys to get a look into your bag and at the ball you were playing. I think he did his checks during practice rounds, though, when the players didn't mind using what they endorsed. The players got to know his gambits and could fool him much of the time. When Eddie died, his wife took over his job. I don't envy her.

I don't know many people who can tell the difference in balls and clubs if they have the wrong markings on them anyway. A player takes another manufacturer's club to his own company and asks to have it duplicated and it is. The player is looking for every tiny edge he can find to win tournaments. That's his first worry in life. He worries about integrity in endorsements some other time.

I'm convinced that all modern advertising is dishonest. Do you think car manufacturers don't try to mislead you? There are other keen similarities between the car business and the golf equipment business. Like the car manufacturers, the equipment companies have model years. With rare exceptions the new lines of clubs carry only cosmetic changes, like new cars. But everybody has to pretend there is some startling new technological feature of the clubs or ball that is going to cut six strokes off your Aunt Polly's game.

177

The golf equipment companies get upset with us when we don't take the new line of clubs every year. Many tour pros become attached to a set of clubs or at least a driver. Frank Beard has been playing the same set of Hillerich and Bradsby clubs for more than fifteen years. The company doesn't like it, but in a way Frank is the best possible advertisement for the product. He's been hitting thousands of golf shots every week with those clubs and they've stood up beautifully. Of course, the company would rather sell the average player a new set at least once every couple of years so it can live richer ever after, but the company doesn't have enough money to make the player change clubs every year, because he can earn more than his retainer in a week if he wins a tournament. You gain confidence in a set of clubs. You can have the specifications exactly matched in a new set but it won't feel the same. I'm playing an old set of Spaldings I've had for longer than I can remember.

As far as the tour players and advertising are concerned, the whole false front is unnecessary. It might come as a shock to the fan who plays the game to learn that he may not be able to go out and buy the same clubs I am playing, but if he's smart he'll accept the fact that he shouldn't want the same gear anyway. Ninety-nine times out of a hundred it isn't best for him. Ram is smart to pay players to use a Ram bag with a huge logo. The guys can use it; you don't have to hit a bag.

Most tour players use heavy, stiff-shafted clubs and high-compression balls with balata covers. Most average golfers shouldn't. Let's take clubs first. A stiff shaft is for a strong player with good timing who plays regularly. Everybody else should use a medium stiff shaft or even a more flexible shaft. Then they can get the club through the ball with better feel. Don't worry about your masculinity. You might be better off with ladies' clubs, particularly if you're older. A retired gentleman at my Denver course went to ladies' clubs and started hitting his drives 30 yards farther. There's nothing unmasculine about that. Gay Brewer plays a C-9 swingweight, a ladies' weight. Forrest Fezler and Hubert Green swing D-0. Jack Nicklaus swings a light club. The swingweights on the tour range all the way up to J.C. Snead's D-9, which is like a telephone pole. But J. C. is strong enough to swing a telephone pole and you and I aren't. I swing D-2 or D-3. You, the reader, probably don't need anything heavier than D-0 at the most.

Gary Player is one of the few good players I have seen who plays with clubs that are too light. Gary is little, but he's strong and well-coordinated. He can swing the hell out of a golf club. But Gary has always fought a severe hook. When he releases into the ball too soon because his clubs are too light, he gets quick-hooks. David Graham had the same problem but solved it by switching from D-0 swingweight to D-6.

Graham, Arnold Palmer, and I are the most fanatical experimenters with clubs. Among us we have to have 300 full sets of clubs in garages, basements, and attics. We're always trying different combinations of specifications. Arnold has a new workshop that could pass for a club manufacturing plant. There are dozens of bins full of clubs, and he has all the modern machinery to tinker with them.

Sam Snead isn't that much of a tinkerer but has the greatest inbred sense for feeling slight differences in equipment. A swingweight point isn't that big a deal. From D-0 to D-1 is two dollar bills on a set of swingweight scales. But you can give Sam a club that's D-0 and a club that's D-1 and he can heft them once and tell you which is which. I don't know anyone else with that kind of sensitivity. Most pros on the tour don't want to spend the time to work with a manufacturer and get a set of clubs that are just right. They don't know what they want to start with and don't have the patience to experiment and find out.

I am very concerned with the loft and lie of my clubs, two specs you don't hear that much about. They can be critical to

179

the kind of contact you make. Do you know what loft and lie you need? You should. Any good club pro should have equipment to check your loft and lie, but many don't because the equipment is very expensive and average golfers don't ask about it often enough. It's worth your while to have your clubs checked.

You can make a cursory check of your clubs' lie yourself. Take your normal stance and address the ball. Have a buddy see if the club is fully soled. If the toe is off the ground your lie is too upright. You need a flatter lie so that the club will be squarely on the ground at address. If the heel of the club is off the ground at address, you need a more upright lie.

When average players bring their clubs to me to look at the lie, I ask them which iron or irons in their bag they like the best. Almost everybody has a favorite club. Let's say yours is the 6-iron. I'll put the 6-iron on the lie detector machine and maybe find that it's two degrees more upright than standard. So I make all the irons two degrees upright and you're happy.

I vary the lie in my clubs from half a degree to a degree flat. In three or four months if I'm leaving the ball out to the right I'll go back to a standard lie.

The loft in your clubs can be checked on the same machine that checks the lie. This is harder to determine on your own than lie. I have developed enough of a sense for club specs that I can take your clubs and tell whether the increase in loft from one club to the next is consistent—that's the big thing with loft. The manufacturers are allowed a tolerance of one degree either way on each club. Without knowing it, the average player can almost wind up with two 4-irons in a set.

Speaking of loft, the average player doesn't need a 2-iron and 3-iron in a set the way a tour pro does. He would do much better with a 5-wood and 6-wood and maybe even a 7-wood instead of a 4-iron. With the higher numbered woods, he can get the ball airborne more easily. So many players are miserable because they're playing groundhog with the ball all the time. They ought to forget the long irons. It's no disgrace not to carry them. I've known good amateur golfers who played with a full set of thirteen woods and no irons at all. Lee Trevino likes to hit a 6-wood, and I don't hear anybody laughing at him. Ray Floyd is a 5-wood man.

The biggest breakthrough in club design in twenty years is the short hosel that some manufacturers have brought out. The weight has always been more in the hosel than in the clubhead (the hosel connects the shaft with the head). By reducing the hosel you can put more weight in the head, where you need it. You will hit the ball more solidly and get a lot more out of an iron.

We've always heard that a shank—that awful-looking shot that squirts straight right off the hosel—is the closest thing to a perfect shot. Small consolation. But the reason it is the closest thing to a perfect shot is that the weight is back there. When you move more weight into the clubhead and distribute it there, a perfect shot is going to be closer to the center of the clubface, where it ought to be.

I have been asked if I address the ball off the inside of the club because that's where the sweet spot is. Not really. A lot of good players address the ball off the heel or shank because it encourages them to start the clubhead away from the ball a little straighter and return it to the ball from slightly inside the target line. Poorer players are prone to swing into the ball from outside the line, which is why they slice.

You hear a lot lately about breakthrough materials in club shafts. You don't hear it from me, though. I thought aluminum was a swindle. It was a fad that lasted about a year and a half. It sold a lot of clubs but I don't know anybody playing with it today and liking it, on or off the tour. The propaganda was that aluminum is lighter and at least as strong. I'm no scientist, but I don't think you can go to lighter

181

materials and maintain the shaft strength you have to have. I feel the same way about lightweight steel. I use the regular "old" steel shaft. It has the best combination of weight and strength that I ever expect to find in a shaft. One company, True Temper, makes most of the shafts for the different club manufacturers and my bet is that True Temper thinks the same thing. True Temper has to keep experimenting and humoring the manufacturers and the public, but I would guess that regular steel was the last real breakthrough.

Graphite? If everybody on the tour would agree to use a set of graphite clubs, I'd pay for them. It would mean a much bigger net profit for me. You might get a few more yards with the driver—though I'm not convinced even of that—but you're going to lose control and wreck your swing if your swing is any good. So you take weight out of the shaft and put it in the head. All that is going to do for the average golfer is lead him to swing more from the top with his hands and arms and aggravate his slice. You really have to "wait on the club" on the downswing and that's just what the average guy can't do as it is.

I haven't always stuck with steel. Gary Player and his manager Mark McCormack made a big deal with the Shakespeare Company a few years ago for Player to use a fiberglass shaft. It was black like graphite and got a lot of attention. Everybody forgot that I was the first to win a PGA tournament playing a fiberglass shaft. I won the Hot Springs Open in 1963 with fiberglass-shafted irons when Player was still in the process of negotiating that lucrative contract.

I played with that shaft for about six months and dropped it. It wasn't a good shaft then and I don't think it ever will be a good shaft, although it pops up again every so often. I didn't like it at all in the woods. In the irons the shaft was good off close lies and hard ground in the West and Southeast. The ball reacted beautifully if you hit down on it the way I like to. But when you got to the lusher turf in the Midwest and the East, the ball would tend to fly unexpectedly. You could hit a 7-iron 180 yards with no extra effort, which sounds great unless you want to hit it only 155 yards. Gary had that fat contract with Shakespeare for a while but he didn't always play the clubs. Oh well. It turned out to be a terrific vaulting pole.

I use standard length clubs. Most pros do. Chi Chi Rodriguez is an exception. He is small but he has a driver that's 46 inches long; 43 inches is standard size. Chi Chi believes the longer shaft gives him a wider arc, which generates more clubhead speed, thus giving him more distance. That all adds up, but I find a longer shaft harder to swing in good tempo. As with graphite, you have to wait on it, and I'm not a patient man. I've noticed that some older weekend golfers are able to regain lost distance with the driver by going to a club an inch longer than normal. If you can time it, I'd say fine.

Investment-cast irons are good for the public, but the good player is having trouble finding good forged heads, which give a more consistent feel. I can tell the difference.

Another equipment variable the public often ignores that I watch closely is the size of the grip. Everybody's hands are a different size and you have to decide whether you need a standard grip or a smaller or larger grip. Your friendly neighborhood teaching pro can help you. I know some men with small hands who need thinner grips to hang on to the club. Some women have large hands and cannot play with regular women's grips, which are thinner than regular men's grips. If the club is slipping in your hands at any stage in the swing—especially at the top—it could be because the grip size is wrong for you. Some top players claim that everybody should play with the thinnest possible grip because the closer the hands are to the shaft the better the feel you will have for the club's movement. I don't buy that. The difference in feel is negligible unless you have exceptional sensitivity in your hands, and it's more important to be able to keep a good hold on the club.

That's why I wear a glove on my left hand: it gives me a more reliable grip. Ben Hogan never wore a glove. He said it detracted from his feel. But Hogan had a perfect grip and the rest of us don't. The extra grip sureness you get with a glove more than offsets any feel you sacrifice. I see baseball players and tennis players wearing golf-type gloves now so the bat or racket doesn't slip in their hands. The average player certainly needs a good grip on the club more than he needs a better feel of the shaft.

Getting the correct specifications in your clubs can make a difference of two or three shots in your scoring, easily. You will hit the ball more squarely and the game will be much more satisfying for you.

Picking a putter is almost entirely an individual thing, like picking a painting. There are almost as many models as there are golfers. Apply the same lie check you do on your irons. Other than that you're on your own. If you have a repeating stroke, you can try to match a putter to your stroke. Personally I never have the same stroke working two days in a row, so I can't advise you here.

I've always been a Bullseye man. I don't like the feel of any other putter and putting is mainly a feel activity. And I prefer a blade putter. The putter that helps me in practice is that funny-looking potato masher with all the sighting lines on the head. You can adjust the lines to compensate for any vision deficiency you have lining up putts, so that if you see a putt as being two degrees right of where it really is, that sighting error can be corrected. I am the world's leading puller of putts. I can pull the ball left of the hole all day long. I aim left. Everybody else aims right, of course. Since I know I aim left, with the potato masher I can straighten out my aim in practice. But under pressure I can pull a putt with any putter known to mankind. And I cannot handle a putt longer than eight feet with the potato masher. I just can't put the bigger stroke on it.

I'm planning to try something different. I'm going to combine what I consider the best features of the Bullseye and the potato masher, by building a flange on the back of the Bullseye and painting sighting lines on it. It can't hurt me.

I should be able to use a Ping putter. It's probably the best engineered, best balanced putter made. It damn near putts the ball into the hole itself. On the practice green I can make everything with a Ping—but on the golf course I couldn't putt with it for all the money in golf. I'm like a monkey with a football. It's just unbelievable.

In balls I've already advocated that you use a Surlyn-covered ball because it will wear better without costing you much, if anything, in performance. I use six balls in an eighteen-hole round, rotating them to keep them as consistently lively as possible. You want the balls to be warm because warm balls go farther; my caddie keeps them in his pocket. The average player will do just fine playing two warm balls in a round and will save a lot of money.

What compression should you use? Ball compression is a much misunderstood measurement. Essentially the ball's compression is its hardness. The higher the compression, the harder the ball—the less it will compress. The usual compressions are 80, 90, and 100. I play a high-compression ball. Most tour players do. It goes farther and I'm used to it.

Most average players would be better off with a lower compression ball. They can hit a higher compression ball farther if they catch it just right, but the 100 compression ball feels much harder. It's like hitting a rock. If you don't hit it squarely, the sensation is like hitting a baseball with the handle of the bat on a cold day. The golf ball gets harder on a cold day and I'll go to a 90 compression ball for better feel. Lee Trevino will drop all the way down to an 80 or a ladies' ball. The way the ball feels on the clubhead can be more important than ten yards extra distance. Also, if a higher compression ball goes farther, it follows that you will slice or hook it more.

You should run a quick test to determine what compression ball you like best. Hit several different compressions with different clubs and see which shots give you the most overall satisfaction. Be aware that one company's 100 compression ball probably won't be the same as another company's. The range can extend anywhere from 92 to 102 or even higher; there is no limit on compression. One company's 90 compression ball might be harder than another company's 100.

There is more variance than you might think from one ball to another in size too. Sam Snead carries a little ring that is 1.68 inches in diameter, the width of the standard ball. Before a round he breaks open packages of new balls and inserts them one by one in the ring. If they drop through, they're slightly smaller than normal. Sam keeps those because they'll go farther. He rejects the rest.

Above all when you're talking about equipment, the average player wants to get the best price he can, because golf is an expensive sport to play. The price of balls has remained remarkably stable over the years—a top-line ball in the 1920s was a dollar—but the price of clubs has soared. I see a trend that could really help the consumer. Traditionally, according to the gospel of the PGA, you couldn't get quality equipment except by paying premium prices in a pro shop. That's changing with the industry's increasing ability to turn out store-line clubs and balls made with just about as much care as pro-line clubs and balls, and with the courts' understandable inclination to rule pro-only policies illegal. It's going to get to the point where the department stores will be allowed to stock everything the pro shops can—and to sell it cheaper because they can do a greater volume of business. In Florida I've seen golf shops in shopping centers, carrying a wide selection of pro-line goods available at store-line costs. That's going to

186

hurt the club pros in the area badly, and club pros are not known for devising imaginative merchandising techniques to combat competition. Some of these retail outlets even hire pros to help fit customers. They do a better job than many club pros, who are primarily interested in moving the stock they have on hand, whether it's right for you or not.

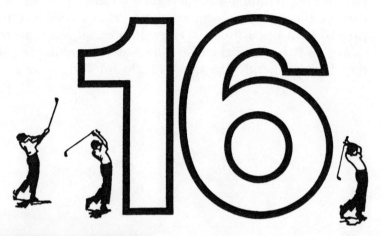

SHOTMAKING

I have always looked on golf as an art form. Shotmaking elevates the game to the level of art. But I fear that the art is going out of golf. The nature of the game is changing.

By shotmaking I mean the ability to bring off all types of shots under all types of conditions. I admire the man who can hit a low fade when he has to or a high fade when he has to; or a low hook when he needs one or a high hook when he needs one; around a tree out of a divot if that's the situation, with the wind or against the wind. There aren't ten good shotmakers on the tour today. In the next generation there might not be any. The old-timers, as a group, were better shotmakers than the modern players, painful as that is to admit. They had to be, for two main reasons.

First, they weren't playing for a fortune the way we are today, and if they didn't become superior shotmakers, they didn't earn a decent living. Nowadays all you have to do to get rich is pitch and putt. You don't have nearly as much incentive to develop a well-rounded game. The young players work on their short games when they practice.

Second, modern course architecture puts a premium on the pitch-and-putt phase of golf. Most courses are ten miles long and ten miles wide, with greens the size of Lake Erie. Brute force is rewarded off the tee, and if you miss a green you aren't penalized.

Skill definitely is on the wane. I don't see anybody on the tour under the age of 35 whom I would classify as a true shotmaker. I see a lot of great scrapers around the green, but they aren't all-round shotmakers. You couldn't put Johnny Miller in the middle of a fairway and get him to hit a 6-iron to the green sliding it in low from left to right, then drawing it in high from right to left. He could hit it only one way—his way—and that's it.

The young players are golfers alright, but not real golfers. They aren't facing up to the full challenge of the most difficult game on earth. Ask them to hit a shot two different ways and they'll put the club back in the bag and go home.

I think the scoring in golf should be changed to preserve the integrity of the sport. I'd give one point for hitting a fairway off the tee and one point for hitting a green in regulation numbers. If you missed both the fairway and the green, you'd have to pick up. I'd give one point for a 1-putt green, a half point for a 2-putt green. A chip-in would be worth one point.

This system would reward skill. The man who hits the fairway and green would come out ahead of the scrambler. Putting wouldn't be so all important.

I'd prefer to eliminate chipping and putting from golf. The man closest to the hole with his approach shot wins. I love the holes on tour where they have contests to determine who gets closest to the pin. That's rewarding shotmaking ability.

I appreciate that some skill goes into putting. I'm sure I'm prejudiced because I'm often a spastic with a putter. But to me it's no art to roll a ball along the ground. My wife can do that half decently. The skill is in getting the ball onto the green. Once you're there it's a completely different game.

Getting to the green, I don't look at the results a golfer achieves, I look at how he achieved those results. You always hear that it isn't how, it's how many. Well, to the professional with an educated eye, it's also how. I look at the kind of shot a man is facing and what he tries to do with it. That's how I measure success on a golf course, for myself and everybody else. I weigh the results against the objective. If a pro is trying to hit a low fade and instead he knocks a high draw into the cup, he still made a lousy shot—and he ought to know it.

Ben Hogan is one of the great shotmakers of all time. His standards are so high that he's usually disappointed with himself, even today when he's hitting balls all alone with nobody else to know what's happening. He doesn't kid himself that he's hitting good shots when he isn't. If he doesn't hit exactly the shot he's trying to hit, regardless of the results, he counts it a bad shot.

A friend of mine recently was watching Mr. Hogan hit balls at his club in Fort Worth. Mr. Hogan had stationed a caddie out across a deserted fairway and was hitting 4-irons at him. The caddie caught one after another on the first bounce, never having to move. My friend remarked that Mr. Hogan must be pleased with such remarkable consistency. Mr. Hogan grunted in dissatisfaction. He was unhappy with what he considered the erratic trajectories of the shots, which looked virtually identical. "There's ten feet difference in the height of some of those shots," Hogan said. To him that is unpardonable, even if the results are outstanding.

That's what I mean when I have the nerve to say golf can be an art. Put a golf club in Mr. Hogan's hands and you have an artist of the first order just as much as when you put a paintbrush in Chagall's hands.

But the art is vanishing from the game. Who can approach

190

Mr. Hogan? Who are the shotmakers? You can count them on one hand.

Jack Nicklaus is an excellent shotmaker. Lee Trevino is a pretty damn good shotmaker. Sam Snead is fantastic; he has great feel for all different kinds of shots. Julius Boros is a good shotmaker. Gary Player isn't bad.

The public likes to think Arnold Palmer is a super shotmaker, but I don't agree. He can hit the low hook but not the low fade. Arnold is a one-way player. It's very difficult for him to move the ball from left to right. He plays with a closed clubface. He plays from right to left, and his left-to-right shot in reality is a push that hooks at the end.

Arnold isn't capable of playing all the shots in the game —he's an incomplete player, like a basketball player who can shoot with only his right hand. Of course, Arnold hasn't suffered that much from not being able to fade the ball. He is still such a good driver that he puts it in a position where he needs a fade only about once a week.

Frank Beard is the same way. He has done nothing but hook the ball all his life, and he's so accurate off the tee that he doesn't need to be more versatile to win a lot of money. Unlike Palmer, Beard could learn to hit more different types of shots. He has a very easy swing with good freedom of motion throughout. It would just be a matter of spending the time.

Nicklaus is the rare player who tries to play a straight ball. He has the ability to bend the ball subtly from left to right or right to left, high or low, but he prefers to hit a straight ball. As somebody once said, that's the toughest shot in golf, and few tour players can manage it day in and day out. It's much easier to work the ball in one direction all the time.

But then that's what greatness is all about, making the difficult look easy. The greatest shotmaker I have seen is Thomas Henry Bolt. He doesn't play much these days except in senior tournaments, but he's No. 1 even now. Tommy is a true artist. He may not score any better than the young players, but he has it all over them in finesse. Where the young players will grab a 1-iron and beat away at the ball with no plan in mind, Tommy can take a driver, choke down on the grip a couple of inches, and play a high fade or low draw.

Let me give you a situation that dramatizes what I'm talking about. You have a long iron to the green and a tree is in your way. The pin is set to the right and there are bunkers right. If you catch the ball really well, you can get it up over the tree and go for the right-hand side of the green.

Most players will take the ball over the tree. Some guys will try to bore right through the tree.

The best shot—the shot Tommy Bolt will hit—is a low fade around the tree. He'll bring the ball in from left to right, completely avoiding the bunkers on the right. If you have that kind of control, it's the safest shot.

The average touring pro just gets up there and plays the one shot he has in his bag and hopes for the best. He doesn't realize that the correct shot is to set it left of the tree and turn it right. He hasn't fooled around with a golf club trying different shots enough to know that there is this higher level to the game. That's the difference between golf and *real* golf, the difference that Tommy Bolt exemplifies better than anyone.

I played with Tommy at Milwaukee one year and I remember a good long par-3 that was about a 2-iron shot. I hit a 2-iron onto the green. Tommy hit a driver onto the green, feathering it in there. The next day, I again took the 2-iron and knocked it onto the green. This time Tommy reached into his bag and took the 2-iron—and put it on the green.

I said, "Tommy, yesterday you hit a driver here. Today you hit a 2-iron, under the same conditions. How come?"

He said, "Well, I just didn't feel as strong yesterday."

That shows the control he has over the club in his hand, no matter what club it is. He can make a driver go 270 yards or he can hit it 230, seemingly with the exact same swing. His tempo is identical, the swing is just as full. Yet he is taking a little off the shot or adding a little to it. He does it by feeling the shot with his hands. He has the ability at the bottom of his swing to burn into the ball with his hands or to soften them as he hits it.

I'm not sure Tommy could explain how he does it. It may be a God-given gift. His high degree of finesse is all feel. Sure, he has refined that feel by hitting thousands upon thousands of shots on the practice range for 40 years, but I suspect he was born with something extra.

I consider myself one of the better half dozen shotmakers today, but I can't touch Tommy. Under pressure, I'm going at the ball full bore 90 percent of the time. That's the easier way to play. Those letup shots are the ones that make breathing an effort if you're in contention on the last day of a tournament. I can play a lot of three-quarter shots, but I can't play the little half shot that Tommy can. I don't have the control to hold back that much and still make good contact.

I play a three-quarter shot to get the ball to go higher and land softer. I make just a fraction of a different move at the bottom of my swing to come up out of the shot a trifle quicker. My extension down and through the ball is not quite as complete, although you probably couldn't tell it if you hadn't watched me play frequently. My legs will move just as emphatically; but I'll shut down my hand speed into the ball just enough to hit a letup shot.

Tommy can stand there and appear to rip a 4-iron while everybody else is hitting a 6-iron, and the ball doesn't go anywhere. He could hit the 6-iron if he wanted to—but he might feel that that day the letup 4-iron is the preferable shot. He's too much.

If you could put Ben Hogan's head on Tommy Bolt's body, you'd see some golf records that never would be broken. Golf is largely a game of patience and concentration, two qualities that Tommy never has had and Mr. Hogan has in abundance. Mr. Hogan never forced a shot he didn't feel sure of. Tommy

193

doesn't have the patience to get from the front door to the back door. He cannot stand to hit a bad golf shot, and if he hits one, it's going to ruin his entire day. Tommy is one of those fellows who if he wakes up mad, he stays mad.

Tommy is about as close to Hogan as anybody. They have an unusual relationship. Tommy has known Hogan long enough to know that Hogan is a human being beneath that cold appearance. Tommy can kid Hogan and call him names, and he says Hogan loves it.

Tommy has told me he believes he knows Hogan's secret to the golf swing. He says Hogan told him he figured it out lying in a hospital bed after that terrible automobile accident he had in 1949. The secret was to weaken his left-hand grip—move it over to his left on the club. All good players fight a duck hook. Once you develop a certain amount of strength in your action, there is a tendency to hit the ball wildly from right to left. Hogan conquered an uncontrollable hook by weakening his left-hand grip.

Tommy says, "Ben asked me one day, real dry-like, if I could use an extra fifteen to twenty yards off the tee. I think he took to me because both of us were raised hard. You know what my answer was. He moved my left hand on top of the club, and after that I knew where I was driving the ball. I couldn't duck-hook it."

Tommy and I share an openness to experiment. The fun I get out of golf is trying to do different things with the ball. That's why I'll drive balls on the practice range twelve hours a day for kicks.

If you work at this game long enough and thoughtfully enough, you start to have a picture of how to play different shots. After a while you can hit one difficult shot in ten. Keep after it and the percentages improve. If you don't learn something every day, life isn't terribly interesting. I have to have the challenge of expanding my golf game.

Experimenting is my nature, and I know it has cost me considerable prize money over the years. I overcomplicate the game, toy around with too many options, and try too many difficult shots when a simple shot could get the job done. Sometimes when I'm playing well, I'll deliberately defy the percentages, just to see if I can prove something to myself.

Take the eighteenth hole at Doral. It's a tough par-4: long, with water on the left side and in front. It's hard to make 4 there playing the percentages, let alone running unnecessary risks. If you take a chance and hit less than a fine shot, you can easily make 6 or more. It is not a hole on which you try to knock your approach shot close to the pin; you just aim for the fat part of the green and hope.

But if I'm going well and have a nice fairway lie, I might get cute. If the pin is in the left rear of the green and the wind is from left to right, the smart shot is to start the ball to the right of the pin and let it stay there or draw in a little. Here I come, though, hitting the ball well and letting my imagination run away with me, and I challenge myself to see if I can bring the ball in from left to right and stop it in the narrow slot left of the pin. I know full well that if I don't get the shot moving from left to right—if it stays straight—I'm in the water. You can't avoid it. Even if I want to knock the ball in the cup, which isn't the way to play the hole, I should start it out to the right and work it in, to allow myself some margin for error.

I am liable to flaunt the percentages and accept my own challenge. Life is more exciting then. I do many dumb things like that on a golf course.

That eighteenth at Doral really teases me. If the pin is in the right rear, then you should start the ball a little left of the pin (but still right of the water) and cut it in. If the ball doesn't cut you're still okay—you'll be on the green. But you don't want to go in there with a hook because if the ball forgets to hook, you're going to be in the back bunker on the right. And from there you're looking downhill right at the lake. The chances are excellent you can blow the ball out of the bunker into that lake. I know—I've done it.

As strongly as I believe a man is not a professional golfer

unless he can make all the shots, I have come to the conclusion after all these years that the secret to winning a lot of money out here is to play basically one way. Hit the ball from left to right or from right to left. You need to be able to make the opposite shot for special situations, but you're ahead of the game if you play with one pattern.

The player like myself who can bend the ball both ways is at a disadvantage because he is liable to confuse himself. When Arnold Palmer gets over the ball he knows immediately what type of shot he's going to play; he is going to play the only shot he knows how to play, that low hook. I might get into a lively debate with myself over whether I should draw or fade the shot, high or low.

The pin is on the right side of the green and Palmer will start the ball toward the pin and draw it in to the middle of the green. He's in business. I might decide the shot is a fade and I want to set the shot left of the pin and work it in. I aim left, but maybe I get my signals mixed up. My mind is thinking fade but my muscles are still tuned in to a hook I hit on the last hole. So I line up for a fade and start the ball left of the pin—and it hooks! It's a big problem.

Most players, day in and day out, consistently do one thing with the shape of their shots. Their minds are clear of all the tactical possibilities that have careened around in my head like bumper cars all these years.

I have learned the hard way that a draw is more desirable than a fade. It's a more natural action and easier to repeat under pressure. You get both more distance and more control.

For ten years I struggled to hit a "power fade." I was trying to get the ball to take off with great velocity and slide to the right just as it began its descent. I was cutting high sliders on every shot I hit from tee to chipping distance. To me, it made sense to be hitting the ball one way. I was eliminating half the trouble on the course. I knew that the ball should go to the right on every shot. My bad shots went straight. I never hit the ball left, so I never had to worry about the trouble on the left side.

I virtually would set up to hit a slice—my approach to a shot would scare the average golfer to death because he fears a slice. I would turn my hands way left on the club amd open my stance way up. I would work hour after hour, day after day, on hitting every sort of fade you can dream of, high, low, a punch fade. The real test was always whether I could choke down on the driver and fade the ball. I didn't care if I lost every ball in my range bag knocking it over a road on the right—I was obsessed with not hitting the ball straight or left.

But that was an unnatural way to play. Whereas the normal swing would be out and through the ball, I was bringing the club in and across the ball on the downswing, to impart a cutting spin. I was almost hitting my left leg with my hands. At the same time I had to be certain never to let my hands release through the ball. I had to block everything with my hands. My timing had to be flawless.

Some days it was, some days it wasn't. Finally I got to a stage when I wanted to cut the ball all the time, but I wouldn't try to if I couldn't do it on the practice range before a round. I could feel during practice whether I was going to be able to cut the ball that day with any consistency.

During much of 1972 and 1973 I went with whatever I found on the practice tee. If the ball was moving from right to left, I went out and played for the draw until I could feel the cut coming. That was spooky. I won at Memphis in 1973 but I was nearly a basket case. The first three days I knew I could only hook the ball. I couldn't cut it the way I wanted. So I played for the hook—but I could never be sure I would get it, I was so used to cutting everything.

I was shooting good scores each day and when I would tell the writers in the press room that I was swinging terribly, they thought I was putting them on. I was dead serious. I was getting away with first-degree murder out there.

How could I win a tour event swinging so badly? I have a lot more coordination than many guys out here. I have good hand-eye coordination. If I feel a bad swing under way, I can catch up in the middle of it, make an adjustment, and get the clubface on the ball fairly well.

Finally, in the middle of the 1973 season, I resolved to play everything from right to left, to draw everything. Harry Pressler, an old teaching pro in Palm Springs whom I respect very much, had been after me for years to hook the ball. At the 1973 Masters, Norman Von Nida, another great teacher, also urged me to draw the ball. Norman convinced me that all the great players from Walter Hagen on consistently drew the ball. Ben Hogan could fade the ball, but his basic shape was a draw. It's a more natural way to play because the turn of the body brings the club inside the target line on the backswing, which sets up an inside-out swing path through the hitting area that produces a draw.

Norman told me what I already knew—that the ball goes farther with draw spin—but impressed it on me by adding that Nicklaus would give up 30 yards off the tee if he faded the ball. Being small and relatively short off the tee, I was easy to sell on that point. I also had always heard that a draw would not land as softly as a fade, but Norman contends that it does land as softly if you transfer your weight well on your forward swing and keep your head in back of the ball.

Norman was staying in the house I was renting, and all day and most of the night I would pump him about swing theory. He has tutored almost all the great foreign players of this era, including Player and Crampton, and is a brilliant golf thinker. After two days I knew I wanted to be a right-to-left player.

Norman warned me not to try to make such a major change in my play the week of a major championship. I knew he was correct. The kind of transition we were talking about, which entails unlearning the habits of ten years, should be done away from the tour and especially away from the Masters.

But I decided to change overnight. A Monday night it was, to be exact. Norman walked around during my practice round Tuesday and went over every shot with me, before and after. The results did nothing to dissuade me from making the change immediately, despite Norman's continued cautions. I shot a 65 that included a hole-in-one at the sixth hole, the prettiest little draw shot you ever laid eyes on. I was hooked, so to speak.

Then the tournament started and the bottom fell out. I staggered through the front nine the first day and stayed near par only through some feats of scrambling that would have done credit to Houdini. On the ninth hole, for instance, I snap-hooked my drive into the trees. My second shot hit a tree and went nowhere. My third shot was a draw that didn't draw—a cold push way to the right almost under the scoreboard.

I hit a great pitch shot over the gallery's heads and sank the putt for a bogey. I was getting it up and down off manhole covers. It's funny—when you're not hitting the ball worth a damn you usually make more putts. Maybe you concentrate better, knowing you have to have them. The ability to recover from trouble is the biggest difference between the tour player and the good amateur club golfer. I can hit the ball all over the course and break 80. He can't.

On the back nine that day I indeed hit it all over the course. On the eleventh hole I hit the first shank of my life. All I could think about after that was the ghastly possibility of hitting the *second* shank of my life. I finished 37th in the tournament, one of my worst Masters ever, and it's a wonder I even made the cut considering what I was trying to do.

Having been foolhardy enough to try to rebuild my game during the Masters, I wasn't about to abandon my plan afterward. I now aim straight at the target or a little right of it. It's difficult. I subconsciously sneak back into my old alignment when I'm over the ball in a tournament. Or I get on the practice tee and find that my old fade is working, so I elect to ride with it; then it stays with me for a day and a half and disappears, and I'm back in limbo.

It takes great determination to make a major alteration in your game, especially at this stage of a career, but I'm going to make it. I'm going to get to the point where a bad shot for me is a draw that hooks just a bit too much. From there it will be no problem to work back to a subtle draw.

I'm swinging much easier for the draw, which should prolong my career. I had a knee operation which set me back some—I guess I'm an athlete for sure now that I've had knee surgery—but now I'm drawing the ball consistently well. My leg and hand action are improved. I'm setting up to the ball with my right knee cocked in toward the ball more, previewing the way it will return to the ball. Starting the downswing, I'm making a more elastic first move toward the target with my legs, which drops my hands down into the "slot" for better control. And I'm releasing my hands better through the ball, again a more natural action than before.

By going to a predominantly right-to-left shot shape, I don't mean to downplay the value I put on shotmaking. You have to have the left-to-right shot for a tee ball on a hole that doglegs sharply to the right, or to come into a green that has severe trouble on the right and a pin position to that side.

I want to be able to do what Hogan was able to do; draw or fade the ball from the same swing plane. When I can do that I'll know I'm a golfer and not just a golf player.

In the meantime I hate to see the game moving away from finesse. I see guys out here making a ton of money hitting it absolutely sideways. About 75 percent of them. They don't know any more about hitting the ball than I do about flying a 747. The tour is getting to be a putting contest.

But there's always the individual challenge of making the ball do what you want it to. That's what keeps me going. That's why golf is an art form. That's why I wouldn't change places with these rich young players for all the money in Fort Knox.

INSTRUCTION _____

Mr. Hogan was the most consistent player in history, mainly because he never broke the plane. The plane is broken when you move the club above it at the top of the swing. Then you force the club out over the ball on the downswing with your right shoulder and right arm.

This problem of coming over the top of the ball is the most common fault of the average golfer—he breaks the plane.

You find your correct plane by addressing the ball with your feet together, keeping your wrists firm and swinging the club to the top. A perfect plane is 45 degrees, which would run from the ball through the top of your spine. Once you have found your plane, the key is to keep the hands and club on the plane or just under it. Don't let the hands or clubhead go above the plane.

The major difference between the pro and the weekend golfer is the first move at the start of the downswing. The weekender starts down too fast with his right shoulder and arm. His legs don't move. The good player starts the downswing with the left hip, sliding it toward the target (the slide soon becomes a turn). He transfers his weight from his right side to his left even before his upper body has finished its backswing turn!

The move with the left hip drops the club into what the pros call "the slot." The club is dropped slightly down inside the plane so that it becomes almost impossible to come over the top of the shot. You will swing the club down into the ball from inside the target line and get power and direction.

Hogan dropped the club off the plane at the top of his swing with a super move onto his left side. He smoothly transferred his weight toward the target with his left leg. His downswing was flatter than his backswing. All great players drop the club some at the top.

Try to stand behind a good player at a tour event, looking down the target line. Watch what happens at the top of the swing. The hands and club don't move out in front of the right shoulder on the downswing. They stay inside, under the plane.

Now move around and face the player. You can really only analyze one thing at a time in a golf swing. Try to figure out what the first move back toward the ball is. I think you always will find that the legs drive toward the target and drop the club into "the slot"—into good hitting position. You drop the club with the left hip, by transferring your weight.

You can't play this game well with dead legs. It's a legs game at the pro level. When I'm playing well I have the feeling I'm running right out from under my upper body on the downswing.

A lot of weekend golfers have poor legwork because they address the ball with more weight on their left side than on the right. Then they have to make a big weight shift back and forth to get decent contact. I prefer to start my swing with 70 percent of my weight on my right side. Then I don't have to worry about moving it there on my backswing; the shift probably would cause me to sway off the ball.

I simply swing the club to the top and drive with my legs from there. If you have trouble getting off your right side at the start of your downswing, practice walking with the shot. Take a step toward the hole with your follow through. You might fall backward instead, a sure sign you aren't transferring your weight correctly.

The average golfer slices, and he does so because he breaks the plane at the top by using his right shoulder and arm to start down instead of his left leg. If you want to stop slicing, start down with your left leg and your club will be in better position. A good arm swing and shoulder turn give your legs time to work naturally.

I'm unique on the tour for my quick pickup. I set the club on the plane by cocking my wrists very quickly at the outset of my swing. That way it has a greater chance of staying on plane. It's a highly unorthodox move that other good players seem to be coming around to. We always hear that we should make a "one-piece" takeaway—the club, hands, and arms all move away from the ball as a solid unit, and the wrists don't cock (or hinge) until late in the backswing. Well, my wrists cock almost immediately on my backswing. I have my wrists virtually fully cocked before my hands have moved back two feet. Hogan also used a quick pickup.

It's a natural move that I've always made. I notice that some of the best and most progressive teaching pros today are beginning to advocate a quick wrist-cock, men like Bob Toski and Jim Flick. They call it setting the angle early—the angle between the base of the hand and the club. The advantage, once you are used to it, is that you are quieter at the top. The club doesn't tend to rebound and break the plane the way it does if you cock your wrists later in the backswing. You have more freedom of motion in your swing. And you're set up almost from the start to make that critical first move on the downswing that we've talked about.

This is about as mechanical as I like to get talking about the swing, particularly with average players. If you get too mechanics-conscious, too position-conscious, you forget that the golf swing is supposed to be a smooth flowing piece of work.

Your grip I am assuming to be respectable and it may well not be. If you don't begin with a good grip, everything else you do is going to require some frightening compensations.

You have to unify your hands on the club. There can be no daylight. The hands have to work as a unit. The palms should be more or less facing on the club. Hold the club more in the fingers than the palms, for feel and control. Most players let the right hand take over at some point in the swing, and that's disastrous.

I have had a serious problem with the pressure points in my grip. I hope I've cured it, but it bothered me for years and I don't discuss it to this day. Worrying about it damn near ruined me. I don't even like to think about it, especially if I'm competing. Basically, I always feel that I have too much pressure in my right hand. Grip pressure is a vastly underestimated subject. It affects the swing from start to end.

The average player plays with too forceful a right hand. His right hand dominates his left when the left should guide the golf swing. I have a quick catch phrase I give pro-am partners who have too much right hand in their swings. I tell them to make a "push-pull" swing. Push the club away from the ball with the left hand and pull it down from the top with the left hand.

All the swing mechanics in the world won't help you if you don't have good tempo, good rhythm. Most players, including Dave "Double-Time" Hill, swing too fast. We try to overpower the ball. The ball isn't very big or heavy, and we don't have to attack it. You don't hit it—you swing through it.

If a person could just forget the ball is there and swing the clubhead smoothly through that spot, he would hit many more good shots. I've seen thousands of players who take a great practice swing and then make an atrocious pass at the ball. They ought to hit the ball with their practice swings.

Tempo starts with the takeaway. If you jerk the club abruptly away from the ball, you destroy your chances of making a smooth swing. Once you're over the ball, you shouldn't clutter your mind with any thought except starting the club away smoothly. Everything else you should have worked on in practice and programmed into your swing. If you haven't, it's too late now.

Average players can learn more about tempo watching the tour stars than anything else. The tour players have mechanical faults in their swings, too, but good tempo gives them time to compensate.

I have a problem jerking the club away from the ball, instead of relaxing and letting the clubhead swing back, because I can't waggle. I would like to waggle the club to ease into the swing but I can't. I just give a little forward press with the hands before I start the clubhead back. I don't recommend not waggling: waggling would have added fifteen years to my life.

I try to make my swing as long as possible; that forces me to take the club away slower, because to get the club all the way back I have to make a big shoulder turn. I extend my turn as much as I can. But it's hard for me to take the club away with any kind of rhythm, I'm such a nervous and impulsive person. It's my nature to be quick and I've had to battle it all my golfing life. People are always saying the golf swing is an unnatural motion. For me it's also an unnaturally paced motion.

Too many players don't practice tempo, they just practice swing mechanics. Good mechanics promote good tempo, but not to the extent needed. I often will spend an hour on the practice range thinking about nothing but smoothing out my tempo. I try to swing every club with the same tempo, from my wedge to my driver. Most players, even on the tour, swing harder with the driver or a long iron than with the short irons. They aren't as consistent as they should be for that reason. I alternate shots with a long iron and a short iron to ingrain the feeling of the short-iron tempo throughout my game. I'll hit several shots with a 9-iron, then hit several shots with a 2-iron, making sure to use the same tempo.

When I'm having trouble with my game I'm very particular where I go for counsel. Tour players are forever giving each other lessons. Those lessons are worth just about what you pay for them—nothing.

There aren't four guys out here who know the golf swing, who understand exactly what causes a bad shot and can fix it. Tour pros play mainly by feel. They've hit a jillion balls during their lives and they've worked out a way of swinging the club almost without realizing what it is. They can't tell you what they're doing with the club or why.

I suppose it is admirable that professional athletes in competition to make a living are generous with their advice to each other on the practice tee. Some of it is sincere. Some of it is a psych job. Nearly all of it isn't worth the energy it would take to repeat it.

Who's the best teacher on the tour? I'd have to say I am. Why? Because my basic opinions about the fundamental golf swing don't vary. I know what I'm trying to do with a golf swing and what I believe you should be trying to do. Others are searching for a "secret" that doesn't exist.

I'm glad to work with young players when they ask. I don't volunteer anything because I think that would be presumptuous. I am happy to share my knowledge with other people. I don't want to be like a doctor who comes up with a cure for a rare disease and takes it to the grave with him.

Ben Hogan is a little that way. He knows as much about the golf swing as anybody, but he doesn't come loose with a lot of knowledge. He's an ingoing man. He wrote a couple of books he expects people to read instead of bothering him with questions. Books can confuse you, though, and they're never complete.

You do not sit and talk swing theory with Mr. Hogan for three hours. Three minutes maybe, but not three hours. He doesn't let people get that close to him. He feels that anybody who is interested enough in having a good golf swing will work hard at it and find out for himself, which is what Mr. Hogan did. If he really likes you he might make the game easier for you, but he is a man of few words, all of them carefully chosen.

He was a great help to me through a terse conversation at the old Carling Tournament at Oakland Hills one year. I mentioned before that I went through a long period going out of my mind over the pressure points in my grip. I worked up my nerve and went up to Mr. Hogan.

"Where do you put the pressure in your right hand?" I asked him after introducing myself.

He paused for what seemed like an hour, staring right through me, and then said, "In the middle two fingers."

That was the extent of the dialogue, but it cleared my mind. Like most people, I had too much pressure in the index finger of my right hand. It took me two solid months of practice to get the feeling of what Mr. Hogan had told me, but once I did, I wasn't losing the club anymore.

I would give anything if I could go to Mr. Hogan regularly when something is bothering me. As well as I think I know the golf swing, I can't see myself in action. It's easy to feel you're doing one thing when you're actually doing something entirely different.

I have discussed my admiration for Norman Von Nida. Bob Toski, who used to be a good tour player, has a reputation today as the top teacher in golf. He's worked with a lot of young pros out here. I'm sure he's good but I don't rate him that highly. His ideas change too much. And he's too much of a showman for me. He enthralls students with a lot of theatrics—ranting and raving and moving them here and there—that doesn't have much to do with the pupil's problem.

Henry Ransom, the old PGA champ and former golf coach at Texas A & M, still hits it so straight it makes you sick. He hits it straighter on a par-3 with a driver than anybody I ever saw. Henry is a great teacher of basic leg motion.

He is like me in that he communicates instructions in simple terms that don't confuse anybody. We avoid confusing jargon, like the word "square," which can mean fourteen different things.

Harry Pressler is a veteran driving range pro in Palm Springs who has tutored many of the top women pros. I go to him for help with my upper body action. He knows how to work a pupil comfortably into position. He has a strap he's developed that he puts around your upper arms to force you to stretch and make a good backswing shoulder turn. Harry is in his mid-70s but has the vitality of six men half his age. He teaches from eight in the morning till eight at night, and he'll work just as long as you will.

John Jacobs from Great Britain is a Band-Aid teacher, which bothers some people, but you have to be. You just can't take golfers who have been playing for years and start them over from scratch. A lot of times you have to create a fault in a person's swing to fix a fault. John might tell somebody who is slicing all the time to try to hit four inches behind the ball; that way he won't be able to come over the top.

Joe Norwood in Los Angeles gets good pupil results at his club. And that, in the final say-so, is all you can go by.

The weekend golfer wants a quick cure to his problems. He's kidding himself, but a Band-Aid job can help him play a little better, and that will satisfy him. The average golfer is struggling to break 100, and if you can get him shooting 94, he's going to be delighted.

You have to be born with great coordination to play this

game. Ninety-nine people out of 100 aren't. I was one of the lucky ones. You either have it or you don't.

But your typical teaching pro has a set formula he gives to every pupil. He has one method that he foists off on everybody, in its entirety. He's kidding himself and his pupil.

A good teacher can take what the pupil brings to him and find a quick way to let the man or woman play better. He won't muddle the pupil's mind with a whole system and try to turn a rough charcoal sketch into a Rembrandt. He won't take the easy way out and feed everybody the same material. For example, most average golfers come over the top. You might have to give a guy an unorthodox grip to get him to stop coming over the top. With another guy, you might leave his grip alone and change his alignment. Different strokes for different folks.

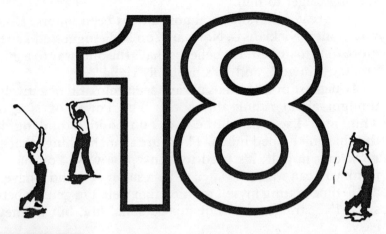

MENTAL

When you've beaten as many golf balls as I have for 30 years, the game becomes 90 percent mental. Golf is the most mental of all sports. You can never stop thinking on the golf course.

I had knee surgery late in 1973 and one of my smart-assed fellow pros said, "How's that going to help his head?" Unless you're a lot luckier than I am, you can't let your natural personality and pace come through on the course. Off the course I'm the most nervous person you ever saw. I can't sit still for two minutes without pacing the floor and lighting a cigarette. But I have to keep myself under control on the course, even though there's no outlet for my emotions. You can't imagine what it's like for a guy with a temperament like mine to keep from throwing clubs and fighting people when things aren't going well in a tournament. My instincts are to hit back—but there's nobody to hit.

Golf really forces you to get to know yourself. It's a lonely game, and if you aren't neurotic to start with, you should be after a few years on the tour. I've heard that's why Bobby Jones quit competitive golf at such an early age. The game was starting to get to him.

The great golfers have almost always been loners. Hogan was a loner. Nicklaus is. Norman Von Nida suggested I spend more time to myself. He believes that's the only way to achieve greatness in golf, and he's probably right.

My biggest problem has always been thinking negatively. I thought about titling this book "The Power of Negative Thinking." I've read all the books on positive thinking, but they haven't helped much. There are so many things that can go wrong in golf, it's hard to think positively. You have to think you can walk on water to be a superstar, and I have an awful time getting myself to think that well. I'm getting better since I've straightened out my personal life, but it's never easy.

Every year it takes me until spring to concentrate worth a darn. People laugh at you when you score in the 60s and claim you aren't thinking or playing worth a damn, but it's often true. A pro learns to scramble and save his pars. He can hit a tee shot that would embarrass a 90-shooter, scrape a second shot into a bunker, but still manufacture a par-4 with a tricky approach shot and a pressure putt.

You have to learn to win money with a bad swing in any given week, by being tough mentally. If you feel a hook, you play for the hook; this can be spooky if you're used to fading the ball.

Putting is what scares me to death. You think the pros have nerves of steel? I get so nervous over a short putt that I shake like a palsy victim. I can think of a zillion ways to miss it. I keep changing putters and changing the way I put my hands on the club. Then I'll have an excuse if I miss.

Putting is Clutch City. I'd like to see the top athletes from other sports face three-foot putts for a living. Jim Wiechers once said putting problems were mental, like Wilt Chamberlain's free-throwing weakness. Larry Stubblefield overheard him and said, "Yeah, but Chamberlain doesn't have to fight those three-footers coming back." That's a helluva difference.

Pro athletes say they don't choke under pressure. If they don't, they're better men than I am. I can choke like a dog.

I remember at Memphis in 1967, when I won, I couldn't get the ball airborne the last day. I was putting well, which is unusual. Usually my putting touch deserts me under pressure. From five feet in to the hole you're in the throw-up zone.

It's funny, but I have dogged many a short putt when I have a *good* round going. There's something about it. You get several strokes under par and your putting stroke speeds up and you get to the point where you're afraid of making a bogey and ruining your hot streak. There's that negative thought that's going to trip you up. Now you start looking for the trouble off the tee instead of thinking about just knocking the ball out into the fairway. You lose your tunnel vision. Pretty soon you're bogeying three straight holes.

You have to be in position to win a few tournaments before you stop getting scared. The toughest thing in the world for me to do is to lead a tournament for the first three days and go into the last round ahead by only a shot or two. You know there are a dozen guys who will go around you if you make one little mistake. You play to protect your lead instead of treating each shot as a separate challenge.

More so than the fans think, it's a game of who chokes the least. The best competitors do most of the winning. Everybody has a little choke in him, feels the pressure. Gardner Dickinson is a hard man and a fierce competitor. Gardner has had surgery on the back of his neck. The muscles have bunched up because he's so tense playing golf.

I have a different theory about how good players can hold up under pressure. I think the man with a fast, hard swing is generally more likely to take the heat than the man with a

213

long, slow swing. The man who has a fast swing tempo doesn't have a lot of room to get faster. But the man with a slow tempo just might speed up when he's under the gun, which will throw him off.

When you feel the tension out here, the most terrifying challenge is to finish your backswing when you have a crucial long-iron shot. It's very, very difficult to make as long a swing as you know you need.

Whenever I get in that situation I tell myself to take as full a swing as I can, to complete my backswing. I choke down on the grip for control, flex my knees a little more to relax, and try to hit the ball hard. Under extreme pressure I forget about trying to hit finesse shots for the most part. I know my nerves probably won't be good enough.

The high, soft, three-quarter shot is too much on the last three or four holes of a tournament if you're in contention. Say you don't think a 7-iron is quite enough club and so you are tempted to hit a letup 6-iron. I prefer to hit the 7-iron harder than usual. I'll hook it to get an extra five or six yards maybe. If I don't think that will get me home, I'll choke down on the 6-iron and hit it in there high and soft, because when I cut a shot I hit it hard.

The trick when you're over the ball in a situation like this is to have your mind made up about the shot. You can't be debating with yourself. Choose a club and visualize in your mind the shot you want to make. Your brain will transmit that message to your muscles. You have to believe that. The way you set up to the ball is going to determine what happens, so get in good position and then just let your body and the club do the work. The golf swing is like sex in this respect. You can't be thinking about the mechanics of the act while you're performing.

I've tried about everything to help my mental attitude under pressure, from horoscopes to hypnotism. I believe in hypnotism if you give it a good chance. I guess Tony Lema was about the first golfer to swear by it. A player like Hogan probably had the power of concentration to hypnotize himself, although he didn't know that's what he was doing. He'd get in a trance out there. Hypnotism can carry you only so far, though. It won't add to your ability. Gardner Dickinson is a poor putter; he says he underwent hypnotism and the next time he played he knocked down every flagstick—but he still couldn't putt.

Then there is pill-taking. It would be easy to blow it out of proportion. You see a lot of pills, but not many players take heavy uppers and downers, not very often. Now and then I will take something if I'm awfully tired and having trouble concentrating. It's hard to enjoy tournament golf under the best of conditions after you've been at it a while, and I'm not one of those players who scores better when he feels bad. Sometimes you need something to get you going, get your heart started.

One veteran player pops enough pills to get himself pretty high during a round. He comes off the eighteenth green flying at about 35,000 feet. I wouldn't trust myself under that much of an influence. I might kill somebody. I've taken Dexamyl, which is sort of an upper that gives you a lift. It's a common drug, often given as a diet pill. Since I weigh 145 pounds I don't need to diet, but I do need a pickup once in a while. Dexamyl contains some Dexedrine and a little of that is all I want. If you take it straight it can really jack you up. College kids take it to stay up night after night during final exams. That won't help your golf for very long, though, and it can soon work against you.

Dexamyl gives you a false confidence. If you're playing well, you think you can play super. If you're playing poorly, you think you can play well. You can't let it fool you. It's easy to keep increasing the dosage until you're a basket case. You need a prescription to get it, but I've never had any trouble because I have a doctor friend who gets it for me.

I never have taken more than two pills a day. Taken that way Dexamyl seems to clear my mind. I might take one about 40 minutes before I tee off. I never eat breakfast, but I might wash down a Dexamyl with a glass of vodka and orange juice and all of a sudden I can face the world again.

If I have a bad ache or pain I might take a bit of Butazolidin. It goes right to your joints and the ache disappears quickly. That's the drug that led to a horse being disqualified from the Kentucky Derby.

In the long run, pills aren't the answer. You have to find the answer in your head. It's a mental game.

Like a lot of other players, I'm superstitious, especially when I'm playing well. When I'm on a good streak, I'll try to have dinner in the same restaurant every night, drink the same amount of booze, make love the same way. I don't want to change a lucky pattern. If I got six hours of sleep Wednesday night and shot a 66 on Thursday, you can bet I'm going to get exactly six hours of sleep Thursday night.

When a close finish is shaping up and I'm in the middle of it, I try to ignore the leader boards and the other contenders. I don't really want to know what they're doing. I put a number in my head—the score I figure I need to shoot that day to win—and if that doesn't do it, it doesn't do it. That takes some pressure off.

I guess you'd have to say I'm a fatalist. Maybe it's a mental escape hatch, but I think some weeks you're meant to win and some weeks you're not, and all you can do is go out there and play your game.

All of this is amazing when you stop to think we're talking about playing a game that was meant to be fun. But when you work at something so hard for so long, it can pretty much cease to be fun. There's a joke on the tour about the old player who claims his mental attitude is still A-1. He says, "The tour doesn't bother me . . . bother me . . . bother me . . ."

What I don't understand at all is the mental attitude of the average weekend golfer. He has no real mental approach. He's out there taking the game too seriously and getting upset when he should be having fun. Man alive, you have your business to aggravate you. Your golf should be your recreation. It should relieve your tensions, not add to them. Relax and have a good time on the golf course. Let the tour pros be the ones to beat our brains out. Leave the frustrations to us.

My frustrations are fewer these days. I plan to play only about fifteen tournaments a year. I'll give them everything I have, but I'm not going to let the tour be a life-and-death matter any more. I'm going to play for the enjoyment.

My second wife, Sandie, is a lovely girl who has given me a much more optimistic outlook. She's convinced me that golf isn't all there is in the world. Before, if I was playing poorly I'd hit several hundred practice balls until my hands bled. I'd aggravate a bad situation. Now I have a couple of drinks in the clubhouse and go home. I don't let it bug me. I still want to win, and I still care about playing the best I can play, but the game isn't all-important with me. I don't take it home with me.

I still get hot if I hit a bad shot, but I look over in the gallery and see Sandie smiling, and I walk over and she'll say something funny. Suddenly the bad shot doesn't hurt so much. She doesn't know golf—but she knows people. I'm no longer a slave to the game, and I like the game and myself a lot better.